A BOY
NO MORE

ALSO BY PAXTON DAVIS

A BOY
NO MORE

Paxton Davis

Paxton Davis
20 Aug 92

John F. Blair, Publisher
Winston-Salem, North Carolina

DISCARDED

LIBRARY
FORSYTH TECHNICAL COMMUNITY COLLEGE
2100 SILAS CREEK PARKWAY
WINSTON SALEM, N.C. 27103

Copyright © 1992 by Paxton Davis
Printed in the United States of America
All Rights Reserved

This book is printed on acid-free paper.

Printed and Bound by R. R. Donnelley & Sons
Designed by Debra L. Hampton

Library of Congress Cataloging-in-Publication Data

Davis, Paxton, 1925–
    A boy no more / Paxton Davis.
        p.   cm.
    ISBN 0-89587-094-0
    1. Davis, Paxton, 1925–   —Biography.   2. Journalists—United
States—Biography—Careers.   3. World War, 1939–1945—
Personal narratives, American.   4. United States—20th century
—Social conditions.   I. Title.
PN4874.D374A3   1992
070 ′ .92—dc20
    [B]   92-16715

For Peggy,
with love

Acknowledgments

A Boy No More concludes an autobiographical trilogy begun in *Being a Boy* (1988) and continued with *A Boy's War* (1990). It was a long project, and in it I was sustained by the good sense and good cheer of my editors at Blair, Margaret Couch, Carolyn Sakowski and Steve Kirk. I am also indebted to Frank Elliott, of the *Winston-Salem Journal*, and Molly Rawls, of the Forsyth County Public Library, for help in finding two important photographs.

A BOY
NO MORE

1

The soldier's fondest dream is that nothing has changed. He longs for peace, as sentimentalists believe, but less for the relief it brings from danger and tedium than for the return it promises to familiar faces and scenes. War is chaos, senselessly disorderly and endlessly unpredictable beneath its tidy simplicities, and the soldier who survives it longs most of all for stability.

That, after nearly four years in uniform, was how I felt the crisp April morning in 1946 when I received my honorable discharge from the Army of the United States at a processing center at Fort Bragg, North Carolina; and that, I suspected, was how the thousands of other soldiers going through the same separation from service with me and before and after me must also have felt. All told, at Fort Bragg and elsewhere, close to sixteen million men were mustered out of the United States Army, Navy and Marines, all of them veterans of World War II; and most, like me, were heartily tired of uniforms, weapons, dirt, dust, rain, mud, cold, heat, confusion, boredom, dread and second lieutenants unable to find the latrine without a map, and most were as eager as I to regain the sweetness, calm and order we knew civilian life must bring.

My father and mother, along with my boyhood friend Tommy Speas, had driven to Fort Bragg to get me, and in fact drew up at precisely the moment I saluted for the last time, received my discharge papers and walked down the outdoor ramp a free man at last. I was with them almost at once, shocked from even a hundred feet at how gray they'd both become since I left home in 1942. They smiled as warmly and moved as briskly as ever, and their clothes were as trim and fashionable as I remembered; yet something about them—the grayer hair, the paler cheeks, the weariness in their eyes—made it clear they had aged. It did not occur to me, at least immediately, that my absence and peril were a major part of the cause, nor that after four eventful years I might seem as changed to them as they seemed to me. Yet changed I was, far more than they: at nearly twenty-one I'd added two inches to my height, fifteen pounds to my weight, and though I was still reedy and gangly and far from husky I'd completely outgrown the few prewar clothes hanging in my closet and was no longer the adolescent shrimp I'd been when I entered the army. Other, profounder changes in me were less visible.

But such thoughts were far from my conscious mind as we drove west toward Winston-Salem, where we lived, through the bright spring morning. At first we talked about my month-long return from India aboard the troopship *Marine Jumper*, then the details of my five-day rail journey to North Carolina and the tightly planned four-day program through which the army and I had parted company. That was boring stuff to me, however, and I turned with relief to Tommy, who'd reverted to civilian life months before after Signal Corps service in Europe; most of all I wanted to know everything that was happening at home: what all our old friends from boyhood and high school were doing, who was back in college and where, who were dating which girls, where the parties were and, last, what the news was from Freddy.

Freddy Speas, the youngest of Tommy's four older brothers, was our boyhood guru. Three years our senior, he'd invented and organized most of our indoor and outdoor activities and adventures, from a flourishing detective agency in the Speases' basement to "maneuvers" in the deep woods of our quiet suburban neighborhood, from scientific research in the "laboratory" at the opposite corner of the same basement to the Ravens, our backyard football team, undefeated if not wholly unbloodied; at Ravens' games, by Freddy's edict, everyone played even if tiny and incompetent, as I was, and even if it meant putting anywhere from seven to fifteen players on the field at once. He was a boy of great intelligence, imagination and energy, an instinctive leader whom we followed as unquestioningly as the Round Table must have followed King Arthur; his judgment was excellent, something rare in a growing boy; and to the rest of his virtues he added immense tact and kindness—the unusual sort of boy who never bullied or misled his younger friends. But since 1943 he'd been critically, dangerously ill, rallying throughout the war from one collapse only to suffer another.

The problem was leukemia, acute lymphocytic leukemia, a malignancy of the bloodstream about which relatively little was then known. In the spring of his final year at Davidson College he'd been on the point of entering the Bowman Gray School of Medicine in Winston-Salem when a routine physical examination for the United States Naval Reserve uncovered the presence of the incriminating cells, and further tests had confirmed the diagnosis. The influence and prompt intervention of his father, a prominent ophthalmologist, had gained his admission to the foremost cancer center in the United

States, New York's Manhattan Memorial Hospital (now Sloan-Kettering) and immediate introduction of experimental radiation and chemotherapy; but in 1943 most forms of cancer were still diseases of infinite mystery for which the medical wisdom of the day offered neither cure nor palliative. The prognosis was grave.

Yet Freddy was young, robust and courageous, and those qualities had given him a determination that not only sustained him throughout round after round of primitive, often sickening treatment but kept him in good standing at medical school; and though by the spring of 1946 he'd lost nearly a year's work to his disease he was still alive, still comparatively vigorous and still in full-time attendance, by then making daily clinical rounds at North Carolina Baptist Hospital between increasingly frequent flights to New York and more chemicals. All through the war I'd kept close touch with him by mail, for he was a conscientious correspondent who'd grown acutely embarrassed by his civilian status and who, compensating needlessly, had devoted himself to writing his boyhood friends nearly weekly; and I'd looked forward to his long, gossipy, invariably cheerful letters—in which he never mentioned his illness beyond reporting his trips to Manhattan—almost as much as my parents'. But the prospect, Tommy said, remained dark.

That news was disheartening if scarcely surprising, but

in my joy at being home and free of the army I put it aside; by now I'd seen so many deaths and so much misery and destruction I reflexively rejected the absorption of more; I would think about Freddy tomorrow. Meanwhile the flat farmland of eastern North Carolina rolled past, green and still twinkling in the morning light, comfortingly familiar after the harshness of India and the chaotic overgrowth of the Burmese jungle. We stopped only once, on the nearly empty main street of some small town east of Chapel Hill, where Mother popped into a "dry goods store," as they still were called, to look for pajamas, socks and underwear for me, all of which she assured me were hard to find; when I told her I hadn't worn a pair of pajamas for four years she looked baffled, though my father, who'd gone to France with the A.E.F.—the American Expeditionary Forces—in 1918, chuckled in recognition.

We were smelling the sweet acrid odor of tobacco in downtown Winston-Salem by noon and turning onto Oaklawn Avenue, where we'd lived since 1931, hardly five minutes afterward. I felt my throat catch at my first sight of our Dutch Colonial house, surrounded by oak and hickory trees and all but smothered by shrubbery, set back from the street on its green, freshly mowed lawn, all of it beautifully peaceful and untouched by the turmoil of war and unaltered from my childhood, except perhaps that the foliage had thickened and the grass grown lusher from the relief the war had given them from the incessant climbing and trammeling of growing boys. I had grown up out-of-doors, like most of my generation, and had not gone easy on its blessings.

The house itself was still less than twenty years old, a big roomy place built just before the stock market crash of 1929 with an eye for the ease of a family, but it had acquired for me the smells and textures, the play of light and shadow, of something larger and more ancient—when my parents wrote me overseas that they were considering another place in the neighborhood, an architect's own house designed with great charm and cunning, I'd anxiously, unreasonably vetoed the idea, terrified to think of change in the world I'd left behind. But now I was safe; and I silently walked through the rooms, the living room and library, the dining room, breakfast room and kitchen, then up the stairs to my sister's room, my parents' room, the guest room opposite and at last my own room at the rear, the smallest in the house and the one I knew best, touching a surface here and there, rearranging the bookcase almost unconsciously, immensely reassured to find things more or less where they should be. For a moment time seemed to stop.

By afternoon it—and the reality of 1946—resumed. Downtown I shopped in vain for shirts and ties, discovering that the wartime shortage of consumer cottons had not yet ended, as Mother had warned; whether any of my prewar shirts still fit was moot, since my sister Anne, two years younger, had liberated them to take to Converse College in Spartanburg, South Carolina, where she was a sophomore. It was lucky for me I could wear my father's shoes, as my old loafers had similarly vanished, lost, Mother said, to the war effort. It was another piece of luck that at the Frank Stith haberdashery the only tweed jacket on the rack, a noticeably overdone brown herringbone that obviously no one else would have, was my size, give a nip here and a tuck there; and I took it and a pair of Oxford gray flannel slacks with the assurance that both, after the inevitable alterations, would be ready in the morning. It was a meager haul but at least I'd have something to cover my back, though I'd have to wear khaki shirts till I reversed Anne's liberation and got my white button-downs back. It was pleasant, anyway, to have the welcoming greetings and backslaps of the Stith clerks, who'd been fitting me out almost since infancy; and the Latino tailor, who'd cut and trimmed my clothes for as long as I could remember, gave me a huge bear hug and told me he was proud of me. I was proud of myself, truth to tell, though not so proud when I automatically started to salute a second lieutenant on the street, then aborted midway, raising a baleful look from the shavetail—until he spotted the golden emblem of discharge sewn above my right upper blouse pocket, the "ruptured duck" of postwar legend, and grinned with what I took to be envy. It surprised me, in fact, to see how many men on the street were still in uniform: either they were having as much trouble finding mufti as I was or demobilization was lumbering along as slowly as it seemed.

That evening, stuffed on the stuffed peppers I'd demanded for dinner, I picked up Tommy and we went looking for our girls—militant feminism's condemnation of such usage being still two decades ahead. His, whom he would marry a couple of years later, was named Ruth; they'd met since his return and already were thick. My romance was chancier. I'd seen Nancy Smitherman steadily since our last year at R. J. Reynolds High School, but my single year at the Virginia Military Institute, while she was at the Women's College of the University of North Carolina, plus my years away at war had strained our affections; even more to the point was my restlessness. I was unsettled, uncertain, bewildered by the choices and opportunities war's end afforded. I wanted to be a doctor, but didn't; I wanted to write, but didn't; my head spun with extravagant fantasies of adventure and accomplishment, but they were as formless as a schoolboy's. Tommy, by contrast, was steady and composed and understood both himself and what he wanted from his life. I understood neither, and my courtship of Nancy, carried on by mail from Burma, suffered because of it. I was confident I loved her but as ignorant of what that meant as I was incapable of imagining a domestic—or any other—future.

She lived in Ardmore, a neighborhood a mile or two away, and as I mounted the steps my heart began to pound. Her father came to the door, we shook hands and as he turned to call her she suddenly appeared from the rear of the house, as glowingly pretty, with her startling blue eyes and soft brown hair, as I'd pictured her a thousand times. Her smile made my knees buckle. But I was too self-conscious to do what I should've done and instead choked and looked away.

"I thought you'd be out of uniform by now."

"No clothes I could get into."

"Your ribbons look nice."

"These are my sergeant's stripes." I scuffed my combat boots against the rug. "Let's go play records at my house," I said finally. "Tommy and Ruth are in the car."

It was the romantic anticlimax of the century. I was less than two weeks short of twenty-one, the stalwart veteran who'd survived one of the ugliest theatres of an ugly war, and instead of acting like Tyrone Power I was giving an excellent imitation of Mickey Rooney. Peace looked less promising than it had.

2

Many Vietnam veterans hold it as an article of faith that their counterparts of World War II came home from their struggles to parades, marching bands and welcoming speeches by an endless procession of their grateful fellow Americans; and this belief is often offered as bitter proof that they themselves were treated thanklessly on their return from the jungles and rice paddies of Southeast Asia. Thankless they may have gone, but their assumptions about the homecoming my generation got is nonsense. Apart from the practical difficulties Americans would have encountered in putting on parades for more than sixteen million soldiers, sailors and marines from all over an enormous country there is the simple fact that we came back in dribs and drabs, from every corner of the world, as transportation, seniority and the needs of the nation permitted. Many who'd fought in Africa and Europe were in civilian clothes again before the war in the Pacific ended; many who were already in the States or had never left were let go easily and promptly; but others were delayed by the tenacity of the Japanese or were just too far away to be brought home as quickly as they wished and had to wait their turn on the troopships plying the broad Pacific. I was among them, not discharged, though I had the requisite "points," until more than eight months after V-J Day, which marked the official end of the war.

I got no parades either, nor welcoming addresses, nor did anyone else I knew; and by the spring of 1946 American life seemed to have returned to normal so completely that for many the war itself appeared already to be as remote a memory as for me it was a distant piece of geography. The China-Burma-India Theatre, the CBI, was so far away almost everyone who'd served there came home, as I did, to the realization that, half a world distant, he might as well have been on the moon. Few seemed even to know where it was except "somewhere east," "out there" where life was—as I was often assured by people who'd never been there—"exotic." I did not bother them with such details as "exotic" tropical diseases, snakes, monsoons and jungle warfare in terrain that would have challenged the stability and health of the most normal, most ordinary young man.

I did not want for welcome, however. Besides my family and the host of old friends and neighbors of my immediate Oaklawn Avenue bailiwick, most of whom I saw within a day or two, I felt great warmth in the friendliness of older people at the First Presbyterian Church, in which I'd grown up, at my father's office at the R. J. Reynolds Tobacco Company and from the laboratory people in whose midst I'd worked, a raw boy just out of high school, the two summers before I was drafted. It was pleasant also to see nearly everyone on the downtown streets recognize the brass ruptured duck in my lapel, the universal emblem of honorable discharge, and nod and smile their appreciation. Then late one afternoon a week after my return the doorbell rang and I found myself thanked, especially and personally, by Arthur Spaugh, a middle-aged man who lived a block over, on Arbor Road. My hunch is that he did the same thing for all the neighborhood boys, who'd literally grown to manhood before his eyes, only to vanish into the darkness of the war; he wanted them to know, directly from him, that their time and sacrifices were recognized and appreciated. It was a gesture of consummate grace.

My homecoming prompted another celebration, a private one. My childhood friend Grady Southern lived down the block, and his father, the president of Security Life Insurance, had promised to throw the lot of us a big dinner when all of us were back. Throughout the war he'd laboriously typed out a monthly, multicarboned newspaper, of his own odd design, to keep us up-to-date on one another and the home front, knowing from his own experience in the trenches of World War I how lonely a soldier could get. But the dinner had waited—and waited some more—for me, who'd gone the furthest and taken the longest to return. Now finally I was home and all of us were summoned: Grady from Hawaii, Tommy from France, Bob Stevenson from Belgium and a prisoner-of-war camp near Leipzig, Charles Speas from Europe, Nick Dimling from a stalag in Poland and I, youngest and last, from India and Burma and the long road to Mandalay. We were up past midnight, stuffed with turkey and steak, wreathed in cigarette smoke, lying heartily of our heroic exploits on distant shores, while Mr. Southern and Daddy, both veterans of that earlier war and thus the only older men allowed, sat back and chuckled, not really deceived by our grandiose mendacity but so happy to have us home safe and sound—no one from the neighborhood had been killed—they'd have swallowed anything.

It was, for a year or two, a veterans' world. Ordinary people, pleased and relieved at winning the war and having their young men back again, were scarcely disposed to count the cost and sought instead, in many small ways, to celebrate victory by thanking the victors. Bocock-Stroud, the Fourth Street sporting-goods store where a whole generation of Winston-Salem boys had bought their tennis rackets, basketballs, cameras and phonograph records, offered veterans free miniature wallet copies of their discharges, complete with lamination, to welcome them home. At the county courthouse the register of deeds made free blueprints of service papers, said to be valuable. The Reynolds Tobacco Company gave away cartons of Camels to veterans who asked for them, and the Carolina Theatre issued a one-time pass to a new movie if you flashed your duck. At some point somewhere north of Myitkyina, in Burma, I'd lost my driver's license, and in any case it had long since expired; but the local state licensing office issued me a new one without examination and without charge, updating it in the process, a more foolhardy gesture, considering my erratic hand at the wheel, than the genial trooper in charge may have realized. Employers announced on help-wanted posters and in classified ads that veterans would be shown priority; all sorts of new trade schools set up shop overnight, everything from barbering and radio repair to plumbing and arc-welding, urging veterans to master new skills for prosperous postwar America and reminding them that their curricula were certified for G.I. Bill educational benefits. The ruptured duck was everywhere, the magic symbol—worn in the buttonhole of a shirt if one went jacketless—that showed everyone, and especially other veterans, that one was a paid-up member of a special, if hardly exclusive, society. Woe be to him who lacked it.

This was petty, no doubt, but it revealed a larger attitude. A salient feature of American participation in World War II, perhaps what most clearly distinguishes it from Vietnam, was that it was as democratic as the government repeatedly claimed: its size, spread and very nature necessitated universal service; and in the end almost every member of the male population between eighteen and forty wound up in uniform—for a time the draft was taking men up to forty-four. Exceptions existed. The physically unfit were excused, including John Wayne and Frank Sinatra, but "fitness" was often loosely interpreted: a few farm laborers and workers in key war plants, medical students until they graduated. Deferments for marriage and fatherhood were uncommon; the voluntary service of overage men with special skills, like my father, who was offered an army commission before Pearl Harbor because of his trucking expertise, was encouraged. For the first time in American warfare women were sought in large numbers for jobs besides nursing; and as Wacs and Waves and Women Marines, as well as flying instructors and pilots ferrying bombers and cargo planes to England, many performed important service and support roles. It was a cardinal principle of the Franklin D. Roosevelt administration to make national service visibly universal: all four of FDR's own sons served in combat, and so did senators and congressmen, industrialists and bankers, lawyers, doctors, newspaper editors and college professors, as well as the urban and rural, middle class and blue-collar class, rich, poor and black. Here and there a few found successful evasions; in Winston-Salem a handful who'd never evinced interest in becoming doctors suddenly turned up in medical school with the accompanying deferments; but we knew who they were and despised them for it. The real result of draft policy, however, was to purge the American war effort of any taint of class or privilege; though not fought on native soil it was a people's war of shared values and purposes demanding shared sacrifice.

This made World War II "popular" in two senses: the vast majority of the American people both believed in it and took personal responsibility, either as servicemen or on the home front, for its immense human, material and financial cost. This may have been good or bad—that it was the "good war" so many called it is debatable—but it was a war of widespread understanding and acceptance;

and this in turn made the homecoming of the millions of men and the thousands of women who'd waged it an occasion of genuine warmth. Few families had gone untouched.

I cannot pretend to have understood such matters consciously or completely at twenty-one, but certainly they underlay the euphoria I felt immediately in the society around me. For a few days or weeks I was even euphoric myself, for like a man freed from prison I was dazzled at how little I had any longer to do at others' behest: I could sleep as long as I liked, rise when I chose, dress as carelessly or as formally as I wished, eat and drink and play when and how and with whom it suited me to. I still had youth's gift for sleeping long hours, and did. Once I got some new clothes I reveled in shirts, neckties and even skivvies of a color different from olive drab. Mother seemed actually to want to fix me the food I asked for, and it had a flavor I could taste. My father, denying both logic and experience, actually seemed to want me to drive the family Buick. There were sheets on my bed, linen napkins on the table, silver to eat with. Hot water was plentiful, towels fresh; I could shave or not, shower or bathe in the tub, morning or night or perhaps in between. I could go downtown or stay home, play tennis or golf, and needed no one's permission. On the streets, in the stores, even at church, people smiled. They looked happy. They were happy. America was happy.

I was not. I was not unhappy, to be sure. I was relieved to be alive, gratified to be free, almost surprised to be home; it was a pleasure to be back with my family and friends, back with Nancy. But I was on edge; I was jumpy by day and began again, as I'd done my last months in India, to sleep in fits and starts, often bolting awake, my heart pounding, from what had seemed the depths of a sound sleep. I flinched or ducked at sudden noises. I found concentration difficult. One Sunday morning at breakfast my hands shook so violently I spilled and broke a coffee cup. A moment later I burst into tears, and only my father's calm, steadying voice, understanding and sympathetic, broke my jag.

None of this made much sense. After more than a year in the jungle of the CBI's North Combat Area Command I believed myself steeled against fear, if not immune to it, and for much of that time I'd worked in a field laboratory on scrub typhus, a task of some danger but hardly the danger of artillery fire. I'd avoided serious tropical disease and stayed fit. I'd had my brush with death but was lucky.

Yet I was anxious. I was quick, testy, abrupt, rude to my parents, cross with Nancy, truly comfortable only with my friends or with other fellow veterans, often otherwise strangers. But I admitted to none of this, even to myself, for it was a fundamental feature of 1940s masculinity that one allowed oneself no emotional weakness or vulnerability. One day, though, at my wit's end, I threw myself on a resident at the North Carolina Baptist Hospital whom I'd known before the war and learned to my astonishment that ragged nerves were nearly universal amongst us vets: we were all having trouble readjusting to civilian life. I was reassured: we'd been gone a long time, seen and experienced a lot that was hard to absorb. Be patient, he told me; I was going through an enormous change.

In those days of little appreciation of the delayed effects of prolonged tension, let alone so esoteric a diagnostic syndrome as "posttraumatic stress," young men of my generation found uncertainty and anxiety difficult either to understand or master, and patience was hopelessly beyond me. Though I loved the America around me I also found it slack, complacent, too easygoing after so much destruction and disorder. Perhaps in some perverse way I secretly longed for the army. I had my puritan streak, after all; and like Nick Carraway brooding on Gatsby's disaster I "wanted the world to be in uniform and at a sort of moral attention forever." As happy as I was to be free of uniforms, regulations, second lieutenants, danger, discomfort and fear, I'd been made a soldier at an impressionable age and some part of me would remain a soldier for the rest of my life.

3

My malaise gradually gave way to the sense that some-how I must make up for lost time. This too—the urgency of the tardy—was endemic. I wanted to romance all the girls, drink all the beer, see all the movies, read all the books and listen to all the music I believed I'd missed during the years of my bypassed late adolescence. My heart and imagination raced to catch up.

That sounded easy but was, in fact, impossible; I did not know then that what was gone was gone for good, and by early summer I was staying up half the night, smoking and drinking more than was good for me and driving the family car too much and too fast. Life seemed once again to be the endless party I felt I'd been unable to attend.

In this I had not only my oldest friends, Tommy and

Grady, but a trio of new ones. Berk Ingram I'd known from childhood and the glory days of Boy Scout Troop 17, Roger Hendrix from high school, but both were a year or two older and lived across town, so I'd seen less of them. Berk, a strapping towhead with a quick wit and rapid, sometimes jerky movements, was Winston-Salem's tennis star of my generation. We'd been on the Reynolds High School team together and once I'd played as his doubles partner, but he was on a far higher level of skill than I, state singles champion our senior year, and might have gone on to a national ranking had he not been badly wounded in the left leg as an infantryman in Europe; now, a prewar year at Davidson behind him, he was going to the University of North Carolina when not squiring the tallest, blondest and most beautiful girls he could find or any of the rest of us had ever seen.

Roger, dark, compact and wiry, with the most perfect teeth in America, was a fine tennis player too, and better too than I, but after service as a lieutenant in the Army Transportation Corps—he'd supervised the loading of my troopship to India, we realized later—he played only for pleasure and was hard at work studying pre-law at Northwestern; he was bright, lively, spunky and invincibly cheerful, and he was as eager as I to make up for the girls and the beer four years in uniform had cost.

Bob Stevenson was a new friend altogether. His family had moved south from their native Philadelphia during the war, taking a big Tudor house two doors down on Oaklawn Avenue while he and I were away; our parents had quickly become fast friends and so, now, did we. He was a few months older and had gone into the army a bit sooner than I, and to a much harsher war: as a rifleman in the 106th Division he'd been trapped during the Bulge and taken prisoner by the Germans, eventually winding up in a POW camp near Leipzig, in whose railway station one night, during an Allied air raid, he'd been pistol-whipped by an angry SS soldier. He'd survived to come home with a bad case of malnutrition, and when his doctor recommended hard outdoor exercise to restore his fitness he'd found a job as a bricklayer, tediously learning the trade till he won his journeyman's card. He was blond, thick-chested and looked to the rest of us so much like the comic-strip hero Steve Canyon that we at once called him Steve, which stuck. The bricklaying passed the summers profitably for him, but his real interest was in drawing and painting, toward a career in which he planned to prepare at the Philadelphia Art Institute, where he'd been accepted for the fall. Despite his amiable charm, good looks and talent he was also, we quickly discovered, almost dangerously absent-minded, tripping constantly over furniture and street curbs and at least once, by his account, toppling half a story from a scaffold while laying brick. He too had a famished appetite for girls and beer and late-night conversation. Listening to us spinning our endless tales of crazy mess sergeants and idiotic second lieutenants, hardtack K rations and muddy bivouacs, Mother remarked that we reminded her of nothing so much as her two Confederate grandfathers going on, in the same tireless way, about Malvern Hill and Gettysburg.

Memories of war may be ineradicable but they can fade—and ours did as the pleasures of that first summer of freedom accumulated. Winston-Salem offered few fleshpots for the carnal excesses we longed for, however, and the pleasures we found were largely innocent. We went to almost every home game of the Winston-Salem Twins, a farm team for the New York Yankees, who played under the lights of the decrepit but beloved grounds of Southside Park. We sat, sometimes as many as a dozen of us, in the bleachers far past first base; afterward we'd have a pitcher or two before going home. Sometimes we'd find a driving range and put away a few buckets of golf balls. If we had dates we'd neck hornily but unsatisfyingly at one of the movie drive-ins just beginning to appear. What seemed at first to promise more sinful pleasures were the weekly dances at the YWCA, which had a jukebox and a dark room; but the girls, most of whom were friends from high school, were chaperoned as closely as nuns, and little beyond a few close dances resulted. We saw a lot of movies, especially late shows at the old State Theatre, Saturday night rescreenings of *Frankenstein, Dracula* and *Casablanca*, irritating the rest of the audience for the latter by reciting the lines, loudly, before they were spoken. One night when Bob Stevenson and I were drinking beer at Staley's, a roadhouse just west of the city limits, a fight broke out across the room and before I quite knew what was happening somebody picked Steve up and threw him crashing through a window at the rear. He returned unhurt and the drunken brawl ended as quickly as it had begun, and when I asked what the quarrel was about he told me an ex-paratrooper had shown the poor judgment to doubt the danger his drinking companion, an ex-marine, had run at Tarawa.

This was juvenile stuff, but it also expressed our grim determination to have the fun of which we felt we'd been deprived, even if having fun proved no fun at all. Other veterans a few years older, and even some our own age, did it differently. Nick Dimling, whose parents still lived next door, had married promptly on his return from a POW camp in Poland, bought a house in Ardmore and gone into business for himself. At the Virginia Military Institute, of all monastic places, returning cadets, some my prewar classmates, demanded waivers to the old prohibition of marriage and pushed baby carriages along Lexington's Letcher Avenue between drill and parade. In downtown Winston-Salem businesses boldly bragged that their proprietors were veterans and flourished because of it. My friends and I were still hardly more than boys, if boys of a troubled and sometimes troubling hardness, but we celebrated war's end with ferocious intensity.

The future appeared infinitely promising. We made plans. Steve was headed for Philadelphia to study art. Tommy, once a Davidson freshman, would enter the University of Virginia. Grady, who'd gone to The Citadel before entering the service, was bound for Furman, his father's alma mater, in South Carolina. I had no further interest in V.M.I. and was accepted by Johns Hopkins for the fall. Most of these decisions, and the altered professional intentions behind them, probably would have surprised our prewar selves. No doubt Grady had gone to The Citadel, as I'd gone to V.M.I., because he wanted to prepare for war, but neither of us had really ever considered going anywhere else; now both colleges seemed not only irrelevant to our new lives but faintly repellent after all those years in uniform. Tommy, following in Freddy's footsteps, had seemed the perfect Davidson man, and all of us expected him to become a successful businessman; instead he was intent on studying engineering. I still planned to become a doctor but was wobbly inside, and Johns Hopkins, though synonymous with American medicine, was also a great university noted for the breadth of its curriculum and the depth of its scholarship. In high school I'd never given it a thought—I had taken it for granted, despite Mother's warning that the world's opportunities were numerous and various, that Southern boys went to Southern schools. The war had changed things for us all. Part of it was time: we'd been forced to consider our plans for the future slowly, to delay decisions, and in the end we'd made them in far greater maturity than adolescence had allowed. Part was travel and experience: we'd seen immensely more of the world and its variety, and we'd done things our lives otherwise would scarcely have necessitated. We were changed—neither better nor worse, perhaps, but irreversibly different—and we saw ourselves and our lives in new ways. Here was a paradox: dreading change, we were ourselves more changed than anything we saw.

None of us was mature enough to recognize this, least of all I, and to understand it was wholly beyond us. The war had made us a bewildering fusion of worldly skepticism and adolescent naivete. In India and Burma, for example, I'd driven a jeep many hundreds of miles over mountain and jungle roads and trails, hacked out by army engineers from hostile terrain, that were among the most dangerous on earth and hardly been scratched; yet once I was home I became as careless at the wheel as the most reckless teenager. I'd taken meticulous care to wash my uniforms and underclothes, yet counted on Mother to see to it that my resplendent new civilian clothes were washed and cleaned. I'd kept my little corner of barracks or tent as tidy as a pin, yet within days of my discharge my boyhood room became a hopeless mess. Despite years of army discipline I came and went with what must have seemed to my parents disconcerting irregularity. I made dates with Nancy, then rudely broke them. I had saved hundreds of dollars from my meager monthly pay and all of the more than three hundred dollars I got when mustered out, yet I did not hesitate to ask Daddy for pocket money and had still to learn how to open and keep a checking account. I resented it when Mother asked me where I was going, and with whom, though V.M.I. and the army had been far stricter and more intrusive. I knew more about the sexual mischief of the American male than Dr. Kinsey was to report a few years later, yet I remained confused and frightened and still, essentially, puritanical. No doubt even the simplest bargain-basement psychologist would have viewed this as a form of long-suppressed rebellion against years of rules and regulations and the helplessness induced by extended regimentation and confinement; but such amenities as psychological counseling were reserved in those days for the seriously disturbed rather than the ordinarily exhausted, and neither self-scrutiny nor self-pity got much encouragement. The result was that for a while I was a pain and a worry, self-centered and thought-less; and so, I learned later, were we all.

These manifestations of delayed adolescence may have been aroused, as well, by the difficulty we had in absorbing the subtler changes we witnessed. On the sur-face, at least, our families, our houses, our neighborhood and our town seemed only minimally altered by time; but we sensed less visible but perhaps more momentous dif-ferences. Most change in our lives occurs so slowly we only notice it when it has accumulated, and are thus able to adapt to it slowly; my generation had to take it in more quickly. Our parents seemed older, and though this was inevitable it hinted, for most of us for the first time, at their mortality. Girls seemed abruptly more indepen-dent: Nancy had worked in the personnel office at the Reynolds Tobacco Company throughout most of the war, and though her manner was as sweet as ever it had an assertive strength I did not remember. Every formerly sleepy college campus we knew teemed with students, the greater portion of them veterans like us. One-way downtown streets appeared, a bafflement. My family's black cook, Emma, who'd been a fixture of our household and seemed inseparable from our lives, a second mother to my sister and me, had left domestic service for wartime factory work and could be lured back to do her sumptuous meals only on special occasions; one of the results was that we ate out most evenings, Mother explaining without any apology whatever that she'd lost her touch in the kitchen, and I found that deplorable. New housing, whole suburban neighborhoods of it— something called "developments"—arose at every edge of town. In Ardmore the North Carolina Baptist Hospital and the contiguous Bowman Gray School of Medicine, where I'd worked summers, expanded before our eyes: new buildings, more students, more laboratories, more clinics, more everything. These were small things, taken one by one, incremental rather than dramatic, but they added up. In my boyhood Winston-Salem had possessed the character of a large small town, and it and its people still looked more or less the same; but, it slowly became apparent, they were not.

No change, subtle or unmistakable, was more harrowing than the change in Freddy Speas, however. I had seen him within hours of coming home in April and several times a week since, but I had yet to adjust to my shock. He had never been robust or stocky, like Tommy, but his vigor and quickness, of mind as well as body, always gave the impression of an intense vitality that his invariable good humor and keen human empathy supported. The good humor remained, and his empathy and interests remained broad—in medicine, in music, in psychiatry, in the girls he dated, in his friends—but leukemia had taken a visible toll. Though he claimed to have lost little weight he looked gaunt, which his natural gangliness accentuated. His skin was the gray of carpenter's putty, his large brown eyes empty of the flash and confidence with which he'd commanded our boyhood adventures. Worst of all was the slowness of his movement. Illness and medication had robbed him of his most noticeable physical feature.

He said little about his struggle, talking instead about his courses and experiences at medical school, where he'd begun his clinical training; but he would speak, if asked, about his increasingly frequent flights to New York for further courses of treatment at Memorial Hospital. He was getting a new, experimental drug called nitrogen mustard, a cousin, he told me, of mustard gas, and he took delight in the irony that two so closely related chemical compounds could be used so oppositely, one to destroy life, the other to preserve it.

I never heard him complain of his bad luck or its apparently inevitable outcome. When he mentioned his disease it was as if he were describing a case seen on hospital rounds. His composure slipped only once. We often went on long late-afternoon walks, sometimes three or four miles, and one gray May day as we crossed the street and started up the hill toward First Street the big stucco house where his friend Aubrey Hanes had lived suddenly loomed above us. Aubrey Hanes had died of cancer a few months earlier. Freddy stopped. "They never found anything to cure him," he said. He waited. "I sure hope they find something for me."

"They will," I said stupidly, and we walked on. War had hardened me to corpses, I thought; but I still could not imagine him dead.

4

The waning of my enthusiasm for studying medicine had been so gradual that I still consciously realized only that the war had left me deeply disillusioned with doctors and hospitals. My longest service had been as a laboratory technician with the Burma field party of the USA Typhus Commission; its commanding officer, Colonel Thomas T. Mackie, had used his position and men so ruthlessly to advance his personal postwar ambitions that, though a youthful and extremely minor figure, I had been severely and permanently shocked. None of the genuine opportunities to further scientific knowledge about scrub typhus, a tropical infection that caused serious problems for troops in Burma, had been exploited despite the presence of a number of gifted physicians, bacteriologists and entomologists or the expenditure of huge amounts of army money and equipment. But Mackie himself had profited handsomely, winding up—after leaving the rest of us high and dry in the jungle—as the first head of a new Institute of Tropical Medicine at, of all places, the Bowman Gray School of Medicine in Winston-Salem; he'd even taken a house, well before I got back, only a block or two from my parents', on Stratford Road. No doubt I was naive to be so affected, but a romantic idealism had always been a fundamental part of my medical aspirations anyway, as it was for many young men and women of my generation, in an era of discoveries and miracle cures, when doctors' wages were still modest and accomplishment, whether as healer or researcher, was the star to follow; and to witness first-hand the unscrupulous pursuit of selfish gain in a profession I regarded as selfless, even heroic, was disturbing.

I was troubled, but I still did not admit to myself that I was beginning to abandon professional plans I had pursued for years; and my intellectual curiosity about the medical sciences remained keen, as—to the extent that I can understand what I read and am told—it does today. So I was pleased and relieved when, a few days after I got home, I was asked to come work again, for the summer, in the Department of Biochemistry at Bowman Gray. I knew and loved everyone there like a second family, knew the laboratories and preparation and ani-

mal rooms inside out; and besides providing an opportunity to refresh my medical interest by tackling new
work the invitation gave me a job and a little income till
I started school in September.

Biochemistry at the medical school—the laboratories
as well as the teaching department—was headed by
Camillo Artom, who was a "doctor" in both senses,
holding not only an M.D., which was by then irrelevant
to his work, but also a Ph.D., which was the vehicle by
which he had entered research. He was an Italian Jew
who'd served as a medical officer in the Italian army
during World War I but been forced, like his friend and
colleague the nuclear physicist Enrico Fermi, to flee Italy
and Mussolini's persecution of the Jews in the 1930s.
The two-year medical school of Wake Forest College
had given him haven and a faculty appointment and
laboratory; and he had been a central figure in its expan-
sion to a full four-year curriculum, its evolution into the
Bowman Gray School of Medicine and its move to
spanking new quarters in Winston-Salem in 1941, all
made possible by the philanthropy of the Gray family,
whose fortune came from the Reynolds Tobacco Company.

Those were the facts, but his real importance, hardly
suspected by lay people, was that he was a scientist of
international stature whose papers in research journals

were awaited and read by biochemists and physiologists in every country in which free intellectual inquiry flourished, and this at a time when scientists of all sorts were fewer and scientists of world repute drastically fewer than they are today. Nothing about him hinted at his eminence, however; I was not alone in mistaking him, my first morning at work in 1942, for one of the janitors. He was tiny, hardly five feet tall and probably weighing less than a hundred pounds, and he dressed with a carelessness that was a function of his extraordinary absentmindedness, though it would be more accurate to call it his intense concentration on the questions and formulations he was turning over in his mind. In a white lab coat that almost swept the floor, the unlighted stub of a half cigarette hanging from his lips, he strolled the floor from lab bench to writing desk to animal room with huge brown eyes seemingly empty of sight, his prominent temple veins bulging as if straining to contain the pressure of his remarkable absorption in the character and function of phospholipids—or, as he called them, "phosphoLEE-pids."

His English was deeply and sometimes comically accented—the medical students' favorite was "heMOglobin"—but at least he spoke it, while no one he and his wife knew spoke a syllable of Italian; and one sensed that his erudition, though highly specialized in science, was based on a broader general culture than most people's. All of that made him attractive, but even more important for me were his kindness and courtesy. He'd been generous to give me a summer job in 1942, when I was a raw, untrained boy whose only credentials were his recent graduation from high school and a keen but unlettered interest in chemistry, and he was generous again when he asked me back in 1946, when I'd gained some laboratory experience but not much more fundamental knowledge. He had a European courtesy, of course, but went far beyond it in his concern for my plans and in answering my endless questions, which must often have seemed woefully deficient in scientific comprehension. Above all, however, and quite without affectation or any conscious wish to dominate others, he set for me a standard of intellectual integrity and manner; he led by his simplicity and honesty as well as his mastery of scientific complexities. He was direct in his inquiries and always strikingly willing to admit the limitations of his knowledge—"I don't know," he would murmur, his eyes as puzzled as a child's—and his leadership was inspiring. He was a beloved figure in the medical school, odd and gentle and curiously free of the competitiveness and careerism that marked so many researchers there and elsewhere; but he was human too, a man of genius who'd retained his scale, with his beautiful, effervescent wife, Bianca, their blond adopted American baby, George, and their modest, "professorish" house on a shady street in West Highlands, a stone's throw from the laboratory, and all the more heroic because of it. I saw that, and revered it; but I did not see, and still wonder why, that his modesty was just as characteristic of medicine as Mackie's megalomania.

He had a novel task for me that summer. During my two pre-army summers I'd done what were really the housekeeping lab jobs—washing glassware, distilling endless demijohns of water, performing routine titrations, assisting at animal autopsies—but now, perhaps in consideration of my army training and experience, Dr. Artom gave me something not only new but untried, at least by him. The development of the atomic bomb had spurred all forms of nuclear research, among them the use of radioactive isotopes as biological tracers. Through his friendship with Fermi and other scientists in the Manhattan Project, most of them, like him and Fermi, European émigrés, he'd been able to win a continuing supply of the first isotopes made available for medical research by the newly created Atomic Energy Commission; and these he proposed to use in his studies of the metabolism of choline, a key chemical component of his "phosphoLEEpids." A tabletop Geiger counter had been installed in the little room set aside for the laboratory balances, and it was my assignment to measure and record the radiation from the many hundreds of samples he himself had prepared from the organs of sacrificed white rats. Less than a year had elapsed since the first atomic explosion in the New Mexican desert, even less since the public revelation of the atomic bombs at Hiroshima and Nagasaki; I was astonished to find myself at the very frontier of contemporary science, at what a later time would call "the cutting edge."

It proved to be a dull edge. Though the accuracy of the procedure was scientifically promising it was also intellectually numbing. From Dr. Artom I received, dozens a day, small round foil trays, perhaps two inches across, in whose bottoms were what appeared to be dried smudges or stains; these were the samples to be measured. I placed them beneath the nose of the Geiger counter, read their numbers in one position, then, rotating them clockwise by the quarter-hour, in three more, recording each reading in a small notebook. That was it, hour upon hour daylong, the only sound in the balance room the clicking, fast or slow, of the Geiger counter, the only movement my lifting, placing and turning the trays. I tried to tell myself what important work I was doing, tried to interest myself in the click-click-click of the Geiger counter, but it did little to relieve the tedium. My pleasure in science did not revive.

This was no one's fault, and many Americans performed daily duties far more monotonous and with less certainty of imminent relief, but I was young and impatient and looked forward eagerly to summer's end. And the laboratory was still fun otherwise. There was much camaraderie, not only in biochemistry but throughout the halls of the medical school. Marjorie Swanson, who'd been on hand before the war, was back with a doctorate from Washington University of St. Louis and endless tales of her work with Carl and Gerty Cori, who were about to share a Nobel Prize in biochemistry. Frances McBride, a local girl, was the department secretary, pretty and cheerful. A bright new high-school graduate named Howard Weiner had my old job washing glassware and was as youthfully sassy as I'd been a few years before. A technician named Traywick, a tall, soft-spoken fellow who moved slowly and silently through the labs and whose first name neither I nor anyone else seemed to know, did most of Dr. Artom's most exacting chemical procedures, while the department standby, Wesley the janitor, a black man whose bad jokes were a legend, saw to everything no one else wanted to do and kept the humor good. Down the hall—the only other department on that dark basement floor—was the toxicology lab, headed by Dr. William Wolff but staffed by seven or eight astonishingly handsome girls, some of whom I already and all of whom I eventually knew.

Many of us had lunch together at one or another of the neighborhood boarding houses catering to medical students; now and then all of us—toxicology and biochemistry together, plus husbands, wives, boyfriends, girlfriends, an occasional dog and George Artom, the only baby—threw vast late-afternoon picnics at nearby Miller Park, splitting up to play softball beforehand or after.

This resumption of the pleasant but ordinary life I'd pursued before the war did a great deal to restore me to something I could regard as "normal." Evenings, almost always in the company of friends who were veterans too, the talk invariably turned to wartime events and experiences, and though this was predictable and healthy, and though most of our stories were comic—if black comedy—it inevitably continued our psychological imprisonment in the tedious world of soldiers and soldiering we wanted so desperately to escape. This sounds darker than it really was. None of us, so far as I know, was having the flashbacks or nervous collapses Vietnam veterans would report in later decades; but our participation in war had lasted longer than most of theirs, and it had all but consumed our most vulnerable years. For one reason or another, however, none of my laboratory friends had firsthand knowledge of the war, and though they were clearly happy to have me back and even eager to hear where I'd been and what I'd done, the war was no longer at the forefront of their thoughts; so their companionship helped me to "adjust"—if that is not too pretentious a word for it—to the welcome but drastic changes civilian life had brought.

Reminders of loss constantly threatened the equilibrium I sought. One day Nancy Nunn, a wonderful girl I'd known in high school and worked with at the lab in 1942, came by to say hello; her fiancé, a classmate of hers at Guilford College, had died in the war, and so had her older sister Rosemary's husband. Downtown I ran into Bill Soyars, the older brother of my boyhood friend Crichton Soyars, who'd died in a naval battle in the South Pacific. At a Saturday-night party I suddenly found myself dancing with Betty Mitchell, who'd been the beauty queen of our class at Reynolds High School; her twin brother, Bill, a fine boy who'd been a classmate too and whom I'd last seen when we bumped into each other on a sidewalk in Abilene, Texas, had been killed in Europe. I was awkward with them all, awkward inside myself. My neighborhood had been spared, but Winston-Salem had not; and now and then, in the privacy of my blackest midnight reflections, I felt what all survivors feel: embarrassment, though not regret, at being alive.

5

One of the summer's other great pleasures, therapy too, was tennis. I had played constantly since 1937, when I discovered it on a wild Boy Scout trip to Chapel Hill and realized, to my gratification, that it was a sport in which size and muscle, both of which I lacked, were less important than quickness and brains, of both of which I had at least a modicum. Since the early 1930s and Freddy Speas's Ravens, a heroic if unorthodox neighborhood football team, I had been an enthusiastic, diligent and wholly fantasy-ridden athlete, dreaming moonily of my triumphs in the Rose Bowl, Yankee Stadium and "the Garden," which, in emulation of the sportswriters whose overheated prose I devoured twice daily, is what I called Madison Square Garden. Alas for such daydreams I was smaller than most of my friends, weak-muscled, light-boned and prone to bronchitis; and though my zeal for sports never faltered I turned out to be a mediocre athlete, better as a sportswriter in my turn than I was as a budding star of gridiron, diamond or ring. In high school I reported in quick succession for midget football, baseball and track, at each of which I proved in equally quick succession to be a dud. Then, as if receiving a celestial revelation, I chanced upon tennis.

I was not, truth to tell, much better at it than I'd been at anything else; but I broke fewer bones, loved the feel of racket and ball and found the other tennis players good-natured and generous and willing, now and then, to tolerate my awkwardness and play me a set or two. I automatically took this as indisputable proof of my rising prowess and persevered in practice. Mostly I practiced with Grady, who though no better was a much more natural athlete, and we passed many a summer afternoon, after closing our drink stand because of the heat, on the baked clay courts of Hanes Park, endlessly—the tiebreaker having yet to appear—playing out sets that ran as high as 19–17. The logic that led us to leave the shade of Oaklawn Avenue for broiling Hanes Park is as mysterious to me now as it was then, as is why we were always surprised, in that glaring miniature Sahara, to have all fourteen courts to ourselves.

Television and big prize money had yet to make tennis

a mass national sport, but Winston-Salem—like Charlotte and Greensboro, the other larger North Carolina cities—was good tennis country. Besides the two fine clay courts at Forsyth Country Club, open only to members, there were the numerous court complexes of the city's Recreation Department—notably including Hanes Park—and these, like so much else in town, got generous financial support from both taxpayers and the wealthy tycoons whose factories had made the city prosperous and handsome. All three white high schools boasted tennis teams, and to their credit—unlike many schools elsewhere—they did not discriminate between "major" and "minor" sports. A letter was a letter, however earned, and a runt like me could wear his big black-and-gold *WS* in tennis as proudly as the burliest tackle wore his.

All of this helped create a lively environment for tennis, producing many state-championship tennis teams and players, as well as a vigorous, ongoing summer program for players past high school, its continuous vitality being most visible in the City League.

The City League was a weekly round-robin team tournament encouraging and enlisting the participation of all the regulars who'd played together down the years; and it helped give my first summer out of the army some of the fun it needed. The four teams, usually made up of a dozen or so players assigned by the Recreation Department, met after work each Wednesday, playing one another according to a schedule also drawn downtown, six matches of singles, three of doubles. Local retail businesses served as sponsors and provided the balls and sometimes even tee shirts appropriately emblazoned. It was all that simple, and no one ever seemed to know or care as we went along, or even at the end of the season, who was winning or had won. The important thing was to play and, of course, to socialize. All of us were old friends, but time and the war had sent us in different directions. The weekly matches of the City League were thus a reunion, not only with my immediate contemporaries but with the older players whom we knew only on the courts: Frank Griffith, an Ardmore fireman; Garrison Reid, who ran a men's haberdashery on Fourth Street; and Jim Stephenson, who seemed amiably mad, drove an ancient car that rattled as it approached Hanes Park and worked God knows where.

I did not play very well that summer, or ever again, but no one seemed to mind. Whatever degree of excellence I'd reached in tennis I'd reached in high school, and that more by will and daily practice than natural ability; and four years away had dulled it. In the army I'd never so much as seen a tennis racket, and my hand-eye coordination and reflexes were poor. Almost everyone else in the tennis crowd could claim a similar rustiness or worse, like Berk Ingram, whose wounded leg was made no better when a hit-and-run driver clipped the same leg on First Street; the injury, however, did not keep him from earning a number-six spot on the UNC tennis team headed by national champion Vic Seixas. Most games showed lost time but aroused little complaint. Playing together again in Hanes Park was so pleasant the quality of play hardly mattered.

Winston-Salem tennis offered further pleasures. North Carolina being good tennis country, other cities and towns fielded leagues and teams of their own, and frequently—though to no advance schedule—they challenged each other to Sunday matches. Usually a single telephone call made the arrangements, whereupon, on our courts or theirs, a pickup team from High Point, say, played whatever team Jim Stephenson could pick up from our crowd, standard team contests of six singles, three doubles. Saturday-night phone calls generally summoned the willing.

I played in several such matches and made several such trips, always in Jim Stephenson's decrepit, noisy old car, all of us arriving battered and deaf but thankful to have survived another harrowing adventure in motoring. I remember with particular affection a trip to Hickory on a hot August afternoon before cars boasted air condition-

DISCARDED

LIBRARY
FORSYTH TECHNICAL COMMUNITY COLLEGE
2100 SILAS CREEK PARKWAY
WINSTON SALEM, N.C. 27103

ing; the six of us aboard almost literally fell out when the doors opened at last, the air reeking of sweat and smoke. We played at Lenoir-Rhyne, a little college whose dirt courts were much inferior to those of Hanes Park, dressing in its gym. I played especially badly, barely winning my singles match and dragging Frank Griffith, the Ardmore fireman who must have been twenty years my senior, down to a humiliating loss in doubles. Ever the sportsman, he never betrayed his frustration by a cross word or flashing eye, and when we'd swallowed our defeat he only winked and said, "Well, that was remarkable."

All of them were like that, the Winston-Salem tennis crowd, and that easy friendship, free of judgment and criticism, was responsible for much of the pleasure I continued to receive, as my tennis game declined from modest mediocrity to bumbling dufferdom in subsequent summers. I saw not only many an old companion from boyhood or high-school days but others, older, whom I might not have known otherwise. They were fine players, but fine men too, and any society would have been fortunate to claim them. Association with them in those first postwar days was the best thing I knew in American sports, and perhaps, despite the many deformations television has inflicted on athletics, something like it still exists.

But I drew another strength from tennis besides its gallantry and good manners, though I understood it only in later years. It was linked to the war and to the army, which like most soldiers I heartily despised and in which I was reluctant to see any merit. But merit was there and it was authentic, and it was to influence my life. Both of my parents were admirably disciplined, thoughtful, orderly and purposeful—their Scotch ancestry, perhaps, perhaps their Presbyterian conviction that one's time on earth is brief and should be used carefully and well. In this they were neither grim nor severe and taught the lesson more through example than precept. But as a boy I had failed, as boys will, to learn it; I was heedless and sloppy, lazy and indifferent to time. A year of V.M.I. and three as a soldier had helped shape me better, but I had misunderstood much of that too, mistaking the imposed discipline of barracks and bivouac, which I loathed, for what was more difficult and more important, self-discipline. The war had taught me that in the end by means of fear and uncertainty, and I was grateful. Unconsciously, I believe now, I missed the need to discipline myself; civilian life and its innumerable amenities were already spoiling me. Tennis, as light and as inconsequential as it was, revived me. I had to try. I had to practice. I had to be on hand Wednesday afternoons. I had to stand ready, if called, to play Sundays. It was all internal and certainly invisible to others; it was both ordinary and elevated; and for a few weeks in 1946 it was nearly the center of my life.

I took pride in my war service, yet was still unsettled. I was—if only inwardly—apprehensive. The world around me, the world of my boyhood, seemed to me random, disorderly, bent upon purposes I had not anticipated and did not understand. I sensed changes I could neither define nor absorb. Though everything looked the same it felt different. Most of this was the inevitable result of long absence, much the universal anxiety of waning adolescence as it nears the responsibilities of maturity; and all of it soon would pass. In the meantime, however, tennis offered both structure and companionship, and I reveled in it. Nor, as it turned out, were the changes I sensed imaginary.

6

My long voyage home from India a few months earlier
had been routine, if dull; but in one respect it had
opened my eyes to something in American life I'd given
less thought than it deserved. Wholly by chance I'd
found myself quartered in a five-hundred-man troop
compartment deep in the hold of the ship. By another
chance I was the only white soldier there.

I was a Southern boy of conventional views. I'd
known Negro men and women all of my life: like most
Southerners I was on familiar terms with the cook,
Emma, who'd been a second mother to my sisters and
me; with the men from Daddy's department at the Reynolds Tobacco Company who came to mow and rake and
plant and prune on Saturdays, Jim and Henry and Will;
with the many servants at my grandparents' big house in

Virginia; as well as with the servants at my friends' houses and many of the other black men at Reynolds. I felt wholly at ease with them all, with Negroes generally; and to that ease, which almost every white Southerner felt, I was able to add the explicitly liberal racial views openly and sometimes defiantly espoused by my mother, who was a founding member of the Urban League in Winston-Salem, an energetic supporter of the National Association for the Advancement of Colored People and a friend of black Winston-Salem Teachers College and many of its faculty and staff. Though no militant enemy of the status quo I was able to regard myself as at least racially enlightened. I liked Negroes; I wished them success in their pursuit of the American dream; and I took racial segregation, in the army as well as in civilian life, for granted. I believed in equality: separate equality.

This complacency was about to end. The compartment of black soldiers with whom I was sailing made me wonder. Most of them had been bulldozer operators, tractor jockeys and truckdrivers on the Ledo Road through Burma. There, in all-black outfits commanded by white officers, they'd lived apart from white troops. So had black soldiers throughout the army and around the world. But troopships loaded up to no such delicate distinctions: you took the bunk that came next, whatever your color. I was a little surprised but not upset. I was, after all, enlightened.

As the weeks passed and we made our way across the chilly North Pacific I began to feel uncomfortable, however—not at being with Negroes but at what I learned from them. I got to know some well, or as well as soldiers do who meet and pass. They had braved every danger Burma held, some of which—the dangers of carving a difficult mountain road across hostile terrain—they'd faced alone. Their service had been as hard as that of soldiers in any theatre of the war, but it had allowed few promotions, few privileges. In return the army had set them apart in bivouacs almost as carefully isolated and restricted as prisons. Now they were returning to a society that by custom and law would segregate them again, would deny them, by custom and law, the special status it was about to confer on those of us who happened to be white.

I must not exaggerate. I underwent no dramatic epiphany, no "Damascus experience." But I did not like what I heard and what I knew lay ahead for them all. I did not like it when a second lieutenant assembling a detail to swab down the fantail put me in charge of a dozen of my new Negro comrades. I did not like it when he drew me aside, once they were done, and complimented me, as one gentleman to another, on my skill at handling "niggers." Was it my accent? he wondered. No, my Southern "habit of command," I told him, citing Henry Adams's famous characterization of Rooney Lee. My sarcasm failed its mission, alas; he had never heard of Henry Adams.

Cocking a snook at a shavetail was unimportant; what mattered was that my month in a troop compartment with hundreds of black soldiers, most of whom had survived a harder war than mine, had shaken me permanently. I could not be certain what kind of world they would find awaiting them; but they had seen much, sacrificed much, and it beggared belief that they'd be willing to accept the white man's Jim Crow rules and ways forever. India, when I left it, was in the throes of a dramatic, often violent revolution separating it from Great Britain after two turbulent centuries; its soldiers too had fought valiantly—if not always happily—to defend a Crown that for all its occasional enlightenment had repeatedly denied them the full rights of citizenship; and though the separation still lay ahead it was clear that the people of India would soon throw off their colonial yoke. Something similar seemed to lie ahead for my new black friends. What form and how long the struggle would take I was not wise enough to foresee, but that the war had made it inevitable I could not doubt.

Nor could I doubt—though I only halfway understood it—what was happening to American women. My conventional upbringing had taught me nothing explicit on that subject, and my family's daily life was "traditional." Again, though, there was Mother's example. Unlike most of my friends' mothers she pursued a perpetual program of human and civic reform, and the reforms she sought included the broadening of women's participation in politics and the workplace. She contrarily refused to accept a passive role on the various charitable boards on which she sat, often irritating her male associates; she spoke her mind on matters of controversy, often surprising them; and she openly and often disagreed with my father, who had learned to value the dialectic her independence forced upon them. My point is that, perhaps without intending to, she had started me toward insights of my own, insights I might otherwise have missed. The secondary status of women was among them.

Yet it required no special insight to see what the war had done with, for and perhaps to women. The extraordinary national demand for "manpower" to fill the armed services had created sudden opportunities for women to fill the vacancies the draft had left, ironically bringing them into the workplace to a degree two decades of political agitation had not. The most spectacular example was the immense flood of women into the industries directly producing war materiel, into shipbuilding, the automotive industry, factories producing armaments and aircraft, medicines and uniforms; less visibly but just as centrally to national life women had poured by the hundreds of thousands into food processing, clothing manufacture and what carpentry, plumbing and electrical work the shortage of building materials allowed, as well as into more familiar places in the offices of business, industry, banking, education, publishing, journalism, broadcasting and, of course, government. Rosie the Riveter became a wartime heroine; equally conspicuous were the two hundred thousand Wacs, Waves, Spars and Women Marines, not to mention nurses, of all of whom the popular song (sung to the tune of "Mademoiselle from Armentieres") asked, "The Wacs and Waves are winning the war, so what the hell are we fighting for?" Nancy had worked in the personnel office at Reynolds from the start; more than one female high-school classmate had served in uniform; the air force's Office of Flying Safety in Winston-Salem had employed dozens of women; Mother herself had worked a more than forty-hour week at the unpaid but necessary job of finding housing for the large number of servicemen from all over North Carolina who spent leaves, furloughs or weekends in Winston-Salem; and few women failed sooner or later to help house, feed or simply lend a sympathetic ear to lonely soldiers and sailors. (Marines and paratroopers, it was said, were rarely lonely.) None of this accomplished complete equality for women in American employment, to be sure, and the jokes sometimes sounded a note as sour as respectful; but it was impossible to miss the fact that, for the first time on a large scale, the nation had sought openly, even desperately, to enlist women in the work required to wage worldwide war. Nor could one believe that, having escaped the box, they'd be willing to go back into it forever.

It would be claiming too much to say that I fully understood such things, let alone that I foresaw their eventual importance. I was still young and intensely self-centered, by temperament already more spectator than participant, and I still did not greatly care; but I saw what I saw. Neither could I make much of the numerous other changes I saw in the little corner of postwar America I inhabited. Among them was the obvious fact that people had more money—and more money to spend—than they'd had before the war. Like everyone who'd passed his childhood in the Depression I took austerity as the norm. I spent what little money I had carefully, saved as much of it as I could, was sparing of the few indulgences my generation was allowed. It was not so much being tight as it was remembering how hard times were, even in my relatively privileged family and neighborhood. People bought cars that lasted, clothes that lasted; they postponed painting or enlarging their houses, took vacations at their grandparents', disciplined themselves to food that, though abundant, was simple and cheap.

I had carried that sense of my society with me through the war, as most Americans had, and the necessary austerities of national mobilization had thus seemed, however regrettable, essentially a continuation of conditions already familiar. That sense had now evaporated. People—though not my parents, who clung to their 1941 Buick—were buying new cars, and multiple cars, as rapidly as Detroit could produce them. New clothes, though available only by fits and starts for a few months while the mills shifted back to civilian demand, were snapped up as fast as they appeared. Something new called a "supermarket," offering only something called "self-service," appeared—and immediately threatened, with its variety of choices and lower prices, the old personal groceries upon which most families depended. Beyond the city limits housing "developments," offering small, identical dwellings quickly built on new construction principles, summoned returning veterans and their growing new families; and, as if to confirm the need, the slightly older veterans we knew seemed to be in a state of perpetually increasing parenthood. What would someday be called "the baby boom" was under way.

The American people were off on one of the great benders that have struck or afflicted them from time to time throughout their history—a bender simultaneously nationalistic, emotional and, in its most visible manifestation, extravagantly materialistic—and even a prim young puritan like me, suspicious alike of nationalistic fervor, emotional excess and conspicuous consumption, could be swept along by its force. The United States had won an immense war against enemies even pacifists agreed were a danger to the world, and won with a loss of life, at least among its own warriors, far smaller than the most optimistic prophets had foretold. The struggle had been long and bitter, however, and Americans could pride themselves, as they did, on their perseverance in the face of strong and able resistance by both Germany and Japan, and they could boast also of the remarkable productivity of domestic industry in supporting their warriors. They were rejoicing too in the sheer relief the victorious peace had brought after more than four years of concentration on war to the virtual exclusion of other considerations and, indeed, an entire decade beforehand of economic crisis and deprivation; millions of younger Americans could say truthfully in 1946 that though they could remember peace they had never known prosperity. Now, as if it were a reward for exemplary behavior, they suddenly had both.

The celebratory spirit in which the country basked

was understandable; it was a symptom, probably healthy, of gratification in survival, pride in victory, joy in the reestablishment of civil life and relief that the long American nightmare, which had lasted from 1929 to 1945, was over. It was good to be happy, to enjoy a modest affluence for the first time and to be able to view the future with confidence. The world had not, to be sure, achieved perfection. Britain and France were exhausted and vulnerable. Germany—much of central Europe—was in ruins, as was much of Japan. The Soviet Union had lost more than twenty million dead and its wartime alliance with the West was beginning to crumble under the weight of mutual suspicion. The United States, though undamaged and prosperous, had postponed attention to numerous fundamental problems, including the future use of atomic energy.

No one wanted to think about them that summer, though. Americans had new houses, new cars, new babies, new clothes and plenty of food on the table. What Henry R. Luce dubbed "the American Century" had begun. I was no different from the rest, and the postwar institution that would affect my life most deeply still lay ahead.

7

By the time I entered the army in 1943 I had completed a year of college, and in any event I would have gone back to college, though not necessarily the same college, after the war. In this certainty, however, I belonged to a distinctly small and privileged minority of Americans. My parents' means made the education of their children possible and their backgrounds and values ensured its central importance in their lives and ours. Almost everyone in our neighborhood was of similar affluence and purpose, and almost every boy and girl with whom I'd grown up knew from earliest childhood that he or she not only could but had a duty to go to college, and most knew which college and what he or she meant to study there. I belonged to a V.M.I. family and intended to continue the tradition; Grady's father and uncles had gone to Furman and so would he; the Speases were Wake Forest men and Freddy and Tommy wanted to be too. Not all of us did so in the end, but our college loyalties were more than mere boyish enthusiasms. All of us could be confident that going to college was as inevitable—and as normal—as church on Sunday and camp in the summer.

We would surely have been surprised to learn that our expectations were far from the experience of most Americans of the time. I got a sour taste of truth in basic training when I discovered that a high proportion of my fellow recruits were illiterate, another shock when I was told I had the only IQ above the level of bare competence in my entire battalion of more than a thousand men. I took neither pleasure nor pride in the discovery, though in the end it eased my war, and sometimes I took pains to conceal the evidence; but afterward I saw the knowledge reinforced by learning that in 1930s America—and, of course, in the America of earlier decades—fewer than 10 percent of high-school graduates received any college education at all and fewer still actually finished to win degrees, and all of that in an era when relatively few children, male or female, white or black, managed to graduate from high school.

So-called higher education—college and university education giving access to the professions and their rewards—was, in short, restricted for the most part to the sons and daughters of the well-to-do, perhaps only by unconscious design. But that classic contradiction of America's professed egalitarianism was about to be undone by the most radical enterprise in the history of education.

The instrument of this revolution was the cluster of legislation enacted by Congress in 1944 collectively called "the G.I. Bill of Rights." The G.I. Bill was, in fact, no single document; its provisions appeared in various bills and extended a variety of benefits to World War II veterans, among them low-interest housing-loan guarantees, short-term vocational training and unemployment compensation ("the 52/20 Club," as beneficiaries dubbed it, since it offered jobless ex-servicemen a dole of twenty dollars a week, then a significant amount of money, for as long as a year). But its broadest and longest-lasting provision, supervised by the Veterans Administration, was the extension of a generous financial subsidy for education, and for millions of young men, including me, that was what we then and ever afterward thought of as "the G.I. Bill."

Both gratitude and necessity had provoked its passage. Throughout history the nations of the world had proved ungrateful for the sacrifice soldiers had made toward their protection and indifferent to their lot afterward—

the begging old soldier with his crutch and tin cup was a familiar figure in most societies—and indeed as late as 1932, only a little more than a decade after their service, America's scandalous neglect of its unemployed World War I veterans had brought on the Bonus March and their eviction from Washington. It was thus partly to extend an unaccustomed thanks to the veterans of a new war, partly to forestall the repetition of such a scandal involving the vastly greater number of new veterans, that Congress acted. Yet of less importance than the motives for its enactment were the G.I. Bill's scope and ultimate effect. Both were breathtaking.

So was the simplicity of the working mechanism. Presentation of a veteran's honorable discharge to the V.A. quickly produced a "letter of eligibility," by which entitlement to educational benefits was precisely calculated: on the basis of total length of service plus length of service overseas the beneficiary was allotted so many academic months of subsidy. In practice this meant the payment of tuition up to five hundred dollars a year plus a monthly subsistence check of sixty-five dollars, to which was added the cost of necessary books and supplies; disabled veterans—and there were many—received higher monthly checks as well as the continuing services of neighboring V.A. or armed-forces hospitals. Red tape was virtually eliminated. Once one had ap-

plied, been accepted and presented one's discharge—
tasks the V.A. did *not* undertake—the college did the
paperwork.

This was, of course, a bonanza for the nation's male-
only colleges and universities, most of which had been
all but emptied by the draft, in many cases to be saved
only by army or navy training programs like A.S.T.P.
and V-12—themselves temporary and subject to peremp-
tory cancellation—by running special service schools
and by the temporary admission of women. Coeduca-
tional institutions had fared better and women's colleges
the best of all, but all had lost faculty to the war effort,
not to mention much of the philanthropy upon which
they depended, and most were threadbare by V-J Day.
The G.I. Bill offered the hope of universal recovery,
as did postwar government research grants in science
and technology, so their willingness to assume the
bureaucratic burden of veterans' entitlements was not
surprising.

The G.I. Bill was an even greater bonanza for its
particular beneficiaries and for the nation. For the millions of poor boys and country boys who'd never otherwise have had the means—and perhaps the push—it
was, after years of war and its deprivations, an opportunity to rise and better their lot in American society; it is
only surprising that so many declined to take advantage

of it, for almost nothing in the nation's history would prove to have done so much to lift so many from working to middle class. (The point would not be lost on their children, who came to regard universal higher education as a natural right.) But the nation benefited too, and on a grand scale. In the immediate term the G.I. Bill provided a hedge against the unemployment and economic upheaval the abrupt discharge of more than twelve million able-bodied young men almost certainly would have caused. In the longer term it developed, whatever the conscious intent, a larger generation of professionals—doctors, lawyers, scientists, engineers, teachers, journalists, clergymen, philosophers, artists—than the nation had ever been able to boast, as well as a huge new class of educated, presumably enlightened businessmen. Here was what would soon become a new American leadership, broader by far in both origins and experience than the leadership of the past, with consequences for technology, the economy, world affairs, medicine, education and the social system that the inventors of the G.I. Bill of Rights could scarcely have imagined.

No one I knew pondered such possibilities in 1946; nor did I. Our attention was focused on the immediate future and what it held, and to none of us, as far as I know, did it occur that we were about to become students in what a later friend, a language professor who taught G.I. Bill veterans, called "the greatest educational institution in history." It is a rare gift to recognize history while making it, however; and just as we'd fought a war of historic proportions without understanding much beyond wet feet and tasteless food, so now we embarked on educational programs that, seemingly conventional in mundane detail, would change not only American education but America itself.

My own choice was Johns Hopkins—The Johns Hopkins University, to give it its proper name. I'd known I was going there since midway through the war. It and Swarthmore, Haverford and Oberlin were the colleges I'd been interested in while awaiting my draft call and to which I'd written for brochures and catalogs. I had finished my year at V.M.I. in high standing, winning the honor roll and academic "stars" to show it on my uniform; but a long army stint lay ahead and a year of V.M.I. was enough. I'd found much to value there, and had entered the army not only knowing its ways but in fine physical condition; my preparation for war was as good as such preparation can ever be. But I was not really a soldier, good as I became at impersonating one. I cared for neither uniforms nor regimentation, for neither the imposed discipline of military life nor the mental rigidity to which it usually led. I wanted freer, broader, more imaginative thinking and people, and inquiry had led me quickly to Swarthmore, Haverford, Oberlin and Hopkins. Then a chance army friendship with Ira Singer, a New Yorker with whom I'd attended technicians' school and gone overseas, brought me at last into direct contact with a Hopkins man and Hopkins virtues. My father entered my application and asked for my V.M.I. transcript, and I was accepted while in India.

I made its acquaintance firsthand soon after my discharge. Ira Singer, just home from China, came for a visit and I went back to New York with him in return. We stopped off in Baltimore in mid-journey, and at Hopkins I made what few final arrangements were needed to effect my entrance in September. I met the registrar, submitted a copy of my discharge to the treasurer and signed on for a dormitory room—and meals—with the housing manager. Members of a later generation, accustomed to multiple applications and entrance tests and to paying astronomical tuition and room-and-board fees, may be surprised at how simple, and how apparently cheap, college then was. I completed the entire thing in less than an hour. Room and board cost less than sixty dollars a month. Tuition was five hundred dollars a year and would stay there throughout my tenure, precisely the maximum the G.I. Bill allowed—and Hopkins, one of the nation's most prestigious universities, was also one of its most expensive, by the standards of the time well beyond the reach of most families until the G.I. Bill came along.

Urban colleges and universities rarely boast beautiful grounds or architecture. The Hopkins campus—called Homewood—was an exception. Though situated less than two miles from the business and commercial center of downtown Baltimore, it occupied what had been in the eighteenth and early nineteenth centuries the country estate of Charles Carroll of Carrollton, a signer of the Declaration of Independence; and indeed his small, perfect Georgian mansion provided both the centerpiece and the architectural motif for the campus. During its early decades—Hopkins, founded in 1876, was a relatively young university—a random collection of downtown buildings had served as what campus there was; but an ambitious program at the time of World War I had established the Homewood grounds. All of the principal buildings apart from the medical school, which was located across Baltimore, elaborated the Georgian style of the Carroll mansion and were placed, in a beautifully wooded setting, around a pair of quadrangles, neither complete in 1946 though the guiding design was evident. Gilman Hall, the central building in the upper quad, was a virtual replica of Philadelphia's Independence Hall and housed the university library as well as the various departments of the liberal arts. Buildings housing biology, chemistry and physics filled out the quadrangle save for one place, which awaited its occupant, and grass and trees filled the spaces between. The second quad, on a lower level and at a right angle to the first, contained the engineering buildings. All of this stood, surrounded by woods and a few green spaces for ball fields and parks, at the bustling intersection of Charles Street, the city's main north-south artery, and Thirty-fourth Street, a dual-lane thoroughfare of apartment skyscrapers, row houses and small businesses. In front of Gilman Hall Charles Street widened around a large statue of Johns Hopkins himself, the Baltimore merchant whose legacy had brought the university into being; traffic went round the statue in an oval, calling attention to both it and the campus it marked and revealing access to the grounds by roadways leading up around a grassy bowl, Carroll House with its ideal proportions standing watch to one side.

It made an imposing but not overwhelming picture, among its effects being its apparent serenity—even isolation—within the busy turmoil of one of America's great cities. It emanated forethought, symmetry and balance, to which, in my passion for order, I instantly responded, reassured in my choice and eager to take up residence.

8

The summers of youth were still long and lazy in 1946, and my friends and I, deprived of that ease during late adolescence, were content to let the hot months pass slowly; but it was time to move on. The summer had proved a period of replenishment, but I needed engagement in larger matters. I'd been an offhand, often unappreciative son and brother at home and an indifferent, often inconsiderate suitor to Nancy. All of them deserved better of me, but my self-absorption, though understandable in hindsight, let me take them all for granted, and because of it my most pressing priority was to get away from myself.

It is among the many merits of a superior education that it opens the mind to horizons of knowledge and speculation beyond the narrow limits of personal experience and prejudice; and at Johns Hopkins—to which, in fact, I'd turned intuitively rather than because of any carefully articulated view of what I particularly wanted or sought—I was about to be offered it. University sessions were longer and more concentrated in the days before the five-day week, the shorter semester and longer, more frequent holidays became the American collegiate norm, and the year began later and ended later than is common today. The Hopkins fall term did not open until the third and sometimes the fourth week of September. I arrived a few days ahead of time to complete registration, look around and settle in. At Baltimore's Pennsylvania Station I found a cab, had the cabby run down my steamer trunk—then a standard part of student travel—and with it strapped to the rear bumper set off, in a manner befitting, I fancied, my station and class, for the Homewood campus and Alumni Memorial Hall, the single dormitory Johns Hopkins then operated.

My arrival was not lonely. A dozen other cabs bearing a dozen other students and a dozen other steamer trunks clogged the tiny parking lot, and as soon as one pulled away another pulled up. The two black porters, Gene and Charles, worked steadily dollying trunks to their proper entryways. Hopkins' urban setting ensured an abundance of rental rooms, apartments and basements on every side, besides which a dozen or more fraternities maintained houses within a few blocks; and in any case approximately half the sixteen hundred undergraduates were Baltimoreans, as required by the Hopkins legacy, and lived at home. Dorm rooms remained precious, however, to the half who hailed from elsewhere, like me, and no bed at the dorm went begging. All but the smallest rooms had gone from single to double occupancy because of the postwar crush, and the ground-floor suites, once coveted for their parlors, bay windows and fireplaces, were now ordinary student warrens cramming in as many as decency allowed.

Alumni Memorial Hall, like almost every other structure on the Homewood campus, was a quadrangle. Its empty fourth side opened upon a large grassy open space in which I was to play much softball and touch football during the late afternoons of coming years. Its central portion, holding the office, commons and dining room, faced the inner court and also contained three stories of student rooms; it was balanced in both directions by matching wings of housing, all done in impeccable Georgian style complete with dormered windows on the third floor, these too coveted for the cubicle-like desk space and view each provided. Six entryways gave access to floors and staircases, but because each entry was sealed from its neighbors there were no long halls or longer echoes. The effect, combining grandeur and privacy, was much like that of the Oxford and Cambridge colleges I was to see a quarter of a century later.

Ira Singer and I were to room together that year, his last and my first, and I found him waiting, surrounded as usual by half a dozen pals and acolytes, on the second floor of "E" entry. Our room, conveniently across the hall from what we all still called either "the latrine" or "the head," proved also to be a convenient conversation stop for anyone needing a shower, relief or merely a cigarette, a crossroads for the residents of "E" entry or indeed any part of Alumni Memorial Hall seeking avuncular advice, which Ira generously dispensed at all hours; his advice was generally sound and covered almost every aspect of human endeavor, so knocks on the door, rarely actually shut, were constant. But I did not yet know what lay ahead, and as Gene muscled my steamer trunk inside I tried to sort out the gaggle of new acquaintances already on hand or arriving after me. One, identifiable at once, was Hank Bobrow, a genial, heavyset senior from Queens who seemed almost as magisterial as Ira; he had been taken prisoner in the Bulge, and prompted by Ira he launched into the tale of the stratagems he'd devised to conceal his Jewishness from his SS captors. With him was his roommate, Ray Carol, a third senior from New York who was, Ira assured me sotto voce, a brilliant student of American politics, a subject Ray proposed, upon acquiring a Ph.D., to teach; he too was a veteran, of the navy as I remember, and he talked out of the corner of his mouth in a hearty blend of street argot and Aquinian logic-chopping. Presently his mentor—soon to be the mentor of us all—turned up: a big, bald, florid Roman Catholic priest, Walter Gouch, middle-aged, paunchy, invincibly Irish and by everyone else called simply "Gouch" or "Tuck," as in "Friar." He wanted to know where we were going to dinner that night. "The Chesapeake," Ira instantly decreed, and without further discussion we set off, leaving the door open, the steamer trunk unopened and a cluster of goggle-eyed freshmen who were *not* veterans.

That note of restless excitement and dead-cert decisiveness was to prove characteristic of my first year at Hopkins, when I and most of my fellow veterans behaved a lot like inmates unexpectedly freed from long prison terms. We were a visible majority of the student body, and in any case probably would have dominated campus life by virtue of our age and our inclination, reinforced by the war, to bully our way to whatever we wanted. Few of us, bringing odd lots of transfer credits for a quarter, semester or year somewhere else, had much idea when we'd graduate, nor did we much care—the G.I. Bill would pay the freight. We intended to howl while we could. The poor freshmen—the real freshmen entering in natural course—had better step aside, which they dutifully did, following us around like worshipful puppies, always good for the loan of a sawbuck or to run out for a pack of Camels.

The Chesapeake, a restaurant on Charles Street not far from Penn Station, was my introduction to the gustatory delights of Baltimore, though I was so intent on figuring out my new friends I hardly noticed what I ate. Ira, Bobrow, Carol, Gouch and I arrived together in Gouch's badly battered old car, but almost at once—Ira having left word of our whereabouts—others turned up. Eddie Kamens was first; he lived down the hall and was like everyone else talkative and effusive. He promptly informed me he wanted to be an actor, then began telling me as he sat down how he remembered Robert Mitchum striding the streets of their mutual Connecticut hometown wearing his overcoat over his shoulders and reciting Shakespeare—a story the probable truth of which was less important than the dramatic intensity with which Kamens told it. He had scarcely finished when his roommate arrived, Horace Hurley, blond, stocky, vaguely belligerent, who told me I must call him "Huck" and complained loudly that there were no Maryland crab cakes on the menu that night. Then a new pair came in: Lenny Scheer, still another New Yorker, small, swarthy, smiling, with the sinewy movement of a panther; and Joe Stefanisko, from New Jersey, wearing the miniature of the Silver Star in his lapel and the amiable, puzzled air of a man who hasn't quite caught the current of the conversation, which turned out to be only too true. He'd been a tank sergeant in Europe, taken a direct hit and escaped with his life, a number of facial scars and badly damaged hearing.

Scheer talked about the Baltimore girls he'd already managed to meet, wiggling his eyebrows; Stefanisko repeatedly turned this way and that to ask, "What'd he say?"; Hurley griped that he'd only come because of the crab cakes; Gouch, Carol and Bobrow argued heatedly about what the Democratic party, which all three fervently followed, would have to do in 1948, what with all the problems Harry Truman was making for it already; Kamens advised me, again with maximum stage business, that the crux of a Hopkins education was to understand "the concept of the concept," which sounded elegant but which I didn't wholly grasp; and across the big round table Ira beamed with avuncular pride in having assembled so lively, noisy and agreeable a dinner party. I said as little as I could, Confederate rube that I suddenly felt myself; but it began to dawn on me, to my relief, that I was not in Kansas anymore.

9

It is a commonplace that the ideal education is the education one has had oneself. In today's educational maelstrom, when the essential elements of a "core" curriculum, even the desirability of a core curriculum at all, are heatedly disputed, the courses required of all undergraduates at Johns Hopkins in 1946 must seem antique. In point of fact they were what the Faculty of Philosophy—the faculty responsible for teaching the liberal arts—decreed to be the central knowledge of "the common culture," which they understood to be the intellectual heritage of Western man. No one pretended that any undergraduate program could convey such knowledge completely or perfectly, but there was widespread agreement, to which most legitimate American colleges and universities subscribed, that it was desirable for every undergraduate, regardless of his ultimate vocational aim, to acquire at least a minimal acquaintance with certain key subjects. Differences existed as to emphasis, of course, and the particulars changed incrementally as time passed; but scholars agreed to a remarkable extent that to win a bachelor's degree worth having an undergraduate should demonstrate exposure to and if possible some mastery of X, Y and Z. To suggest that knowing X, Y and Z might not be "politically correct," or that political considerations could have any bearing on undergraduate education, would have been regarded as an especially contemptible form of intellectual corruption.

Agreement on the canon of desirable common subjects was so nearly universal, in fact, that core curricula across the country—or at least at the better institutions—were virtually interchangeable, in nominal content if not in quality; and the transfer of credits from one college to another was usually simple. Though I gave such matters little thought I discovered at once that my V.M.I. credits had not only been transferred without loss but that every course replaced a similar or identical requirement at Hopkins. I had freshman English composition and rhetoric under my belt and could proceed to the general survey of English literature; my year of modern history sent me, like Johnny Mack Brown running backward to cross his own goal in the Rose Bowl, into a year of ancient history. My German, math and science transferred too, not to mention the obligatory phys ed; and like all veterans I got a few bonus credits for "military experience." Thus festooned with academic credentials, all but the latter on the level, I entered Hopkins as a sophomore.

Soon classes began. Hopkins was swollen with students, but somehow room was found. Because I still thought I might want to study medicine I chose—the only case in which I did so—to repeat inorganic chemistry, and was immediately glad I had. The lectures were given in a huge auditorium in Remsen Hall, the chemistry building, where we sat in curved rows descending to a pit and a lecture bench beneath a large copy of the periodic table. Dr. John Bricker, a young professor of astonishing vitality, paced and wheeled behind the bench as he lectured, his athletic style accompanied by undergraduate whispers, behind notebooks and slide rules, that he'd worked during the war on the Manhattan Project. That was exciting stuff, but even more exciting were the clarity and force of his lectures, which seemed to reveal a whole new way of looking at chemistry. My chemistry at V.M.I. had been adequate but old-fashioned, explaining reactions by "valences," whatever they were; the Hopkins way focused on the exchange of the hydronium ion, on ionization generally, and suddenly, it seemed to me, what had been inexplicable was explained. Here, as Eddie Kamens had prophesied, was "the concept of the concept."

It was fun to be back at the books, and for a variety of reasons, among them relief from the stress of war, intellectual adventure, the company of peers; and like almost every veteran attending college under the G.I. Bill I took an unfamiliar satisfaction in being a student again. College after the war, it became clear, was nothing like college before. I no longer regarded my education as an inevitable privilege, something to which the good fortune of birth entitled me. I had seen too much to indulge that fantasy. Courses were not simply unpleasant chores to be done, well or poorly, in order to rise another rung; they were windows on the world, on life, and they helped explain how the world and life worked, or else sought to. Learning was good in itself, not a duty but a revelation, and instead of a clock needing only occasional oiling a mind turned out to be a bottomless reservoir requiring constant replenishment. Meanwhile, however, I was a sophomore with academic "obligations" to discharge besides English, history and chemistry: two years of French in addition to my transferred German; math through differential calculus; a semester each of political science and political economy. The important difference, a result of war and age, was that I anticipated performing my "obligations" with a pleasure education had never given me before.

My chemistry went well from the start and continued to do so throughout the year, despite my deepening doubt about my aptitude for science. So did history, and under a young professor named Leo Forkey I tackled French with enthusiasm and an irremediably bad accent. Forkey, who wore his hair in a brush cut and strode the campus with military bearing and pace, was whispered to have been with the O.S.S., the Office of Strategic Services, and made two, perhaps three parachute jumps into occupied France—the same story made the rounds a year later about my second French teacher, Leroy Benoit, who was dark and mysterious enough to look like a commando. Both tales may well have been true in that occasionally feverish postwar atmosphere, for almost everyone had been somewhere more or less exotic and done something more or less dramatic; but neither Forkey nor Benoit spoke of such things, which though heightening the mystery left us wondering whether they'd been the swashbuckling heroes we imagined.

I got through political science under Father Gouch and political economy under the fearsome G. Heberton Evans, understanding nothing of the latter but scoring the only A in the course by writing a glib and authoritative final exam on the principles of Keynesianism, the success of which demonstrated conclusively that a mastery of English rhetoric could conceal many shortcomings that might otherwise have proved fatal. Language was no help in math, on the other hand, and I came a real cropper in calculus, never grasping for so much as a moment what a "differential" was or how it could answer, in a trice, the urgent question of when a fly would reach either of two trains approaching one another at speeds different not only from each other but from that of the fly. Nor could I much care, and I ended the course with a dismal—but merciful—C.

The course that most deeply engaged me that first year back, and the intellectual revelation that was to transform my life, was English: more specifically, the required survey of English literature, a perfectly conventional overview, taught everywhere, that ended by altering all of my academic and professional plans. The improbable agent of this upheaval was a desiccated, prematurely palsied and seemingly ineffectual associate professor named Edward Norris, who had been at Hopkins a long time and was stuck for good at a secondary academic rank; he was fussy and unfriendly, a bachelor in his fifties widely said to be a drinker, difficult to like and without visible professional standing beyond the modest responsibility for teaching sophomores a course all had to take but few gave a second thought. But something in the way he read poetry to the large lecture section, and in the smaller weekly quiz section, which I also had under him, made me admire him enormously. He was a routine lecturer, flat and sometimes tedious, and he showed little concern for how his students responded to the material; but I had never heard poetry read that way, easily, conversationally, without the singsong stress on beats and rhymes I remembered from high school, and it gave the poetry itself a new place among the accomplishments that provoked my curiosity. His reading of Hopkins' "The Windhover," which I'd found incomprehensible on the page, brought me nearly to tears with its clarity and force. Yet Norris read without false dramatics or cheap sentimentality, and it seemed to me—though the suggestion drew laughs from those who knew him, and I never heard him utter a word outside class—that beneath his mien of threadbare failure and disillusionment he remained a man who'd heard and been possessed by the genius of the English language.

It helped that almost weekly one of the senior professors in the English Department—or now and then, when it was appropriate, another department—lectured us. Raymond D. Havens, who'd devoted a lifetime to Wordsworth, delivered a moving account of the creation of "The Prelude," lingering with calculated emphasis on the line, "And never lifted up a single stone"; and Don

Cameron Allen, who specialized in Elizabethan and Jacobean literature and thought, lectured on Milton. Kemp Malone, whose international fame rested on his scholarship in Middle English, appeared one day to talk sharply but surprisingly on Somerset Maugham's *Of Human Bondage*, not in those days a novel that usually got much academic respect; and a man named Einarsson, who specialized in Old Icelandic, lectured us on *Beowulf*. Especially memorable for me were the appearances of two outsiders: Elliott Coleman, the poet who ran Hopkins' new writing program, read *The Waste Land*, which was rapidly becoming the bible of my literary generation, and did it with such authority no one clapped, spoke or even moved after he'd uttered the final "shantih"; and Charles Singleton, whose swarthy, bearded countenance gave him the air of a medieval Italian ruffian, lectured us on Dante's *Commedia*, ending with a reading of canto 26 of *Inferno* and the last voyage of Ulysses that sent me scurrying through downtown Baltimore for a copy of my own and, as Singleton recommended, Santayana's *Three Philosophical Poets*. I could not know that Singleton himself soon would be regarded as one of the two or three preeminent Dante scholars in the world.

I was not the first young man to find himself besotted by literature, but—beyond an affection for this work or that—I could not say why it had happened. The origins of interest are obscure, and I had little curiosity about myself anyway. Nor was I especially drawn to writing of obvious emotional intensity, like the poems of Keats or Shelley; though I liked them well enough my deeper attachment was to the muscular prose of such men as Addison, Johnson, Gibbon and Macaulay. In the end there was and is no satisfactory explanation of affinities and aptitudes. Edward Norris was but the catalyst, though a welcome one, for something that may have been happening to me since boyhood. Both of my parents were bookish, literally, filling the house with well-packed bookshelves and always deep in books themselves; and my mother was almost "literary" as well, for she held both bachelor's and master's degrees in English, had taught college English and came close to a scholar's claim of familiarity with the whole range of the English literary canon as it was held in her day. She was widely read, tried to keep abreast of what was being written and wrote a superior prose in her own right, clear, direct, supple and free of sentimental affectation; under different circumstances it would not have been difficult to imagine her as a novelist or poet. My grandparents' house in Virginia, where we spent much of the early summers of my childhood, was filled with books, and my mother and her father and brothers had an ongoing rivalry to see who could recite from memory the longest passages of poetry.

I trod fertile ground, in short, and throve in it from the start. I devoured books as a boy, especially the adventure tales of Dumas, Stevenson, Anthony Hope, Doyle and Buchan; and I wrote all the time, publishing my own neighborhood newspaper, the *Blue Pig*, editing my grammar-school paper, the *Wiley Post*, serving as sports editor of *Pine Whispers*, the Reynolds High School newspaper, as well as covering high-school sports for the *Winston-Salem Journal*, whose inky newsroom I got to know as well as I knew my room at home. I wrote stories, poems, columns, always did well in English; as something to pass the time, and under the disastrous spell of Sinclair Lewis, I wrote an entire novel during a long wait to be assigned in India. I wrote instinctively, automatically, easily; but I was so accustomed to reading and writing I did not take them seriously. I could not think of writing as something people actually *did*.

Now here I was, overwhelmed, a compulsive reader. In the army I'd read constantly too, Maugham, T. S. Eliot, Flaubert, Fitzgerald, Hemingway, Tolstoy, Dostoyevsky, Thomas Wolfe, Raymond Chandler; and a habit had become an addiction. I agonized to Ira and my parents, for I'd believed for years I was committed to medicine. None of them pushed me to go on that way, however, and resistance would not have altered the decision I made anyhow. It came midway through the second semester, dramatic to me though evidently to no one else. Wisely or unwisely I said farewell to medicine and informed the English Department I intended to become a major in the fall. I knew better than to inform them of my pretentious parallel intention to make my living as a writer.

10

Grandiose expectations and plans were not unusual in that first year of peace. "Euphoria" had still to be invented, awaiting a briefer and more nearly bloodless war; but the sense that one's possibilities were limitless was hard to restrain when survival was fresh and the nation, released by a great but hard-won military victory, seemed capable of achieving anything. If in coming decades the United States was to find that cruelly untrue, and if we ourselves were to discover drastic limitations to our own gifts and wisdom, we did not know it in 1946.

Veterans dominated the campus, dominated American life, and the sight of us seemed automatically to confirm the country's most optimistic hopes for its future. We were everywhere, and instantly recognizable by the ruptured ducks or miniature ribbons in our lapels, as well as, less happily, by missing arms and legs or grotesquely scarred faces. Older people smiled and nodded in deferential courtesy, and small boys—not infrequently including freshmen, to whom we condescended with what we hoped was Hemingwayesque disdain for the uninitiated—followed us around.

We were a roughneck lot to be college students, still wearing our G.I. boots and o.d. shirts and trousers as well as battered A-2 flight jackets, tank jackets and field jackets, all mixed with elaborate forethought both to impress professors, freshmen and girls and to thumb a nose at the canons of proper military dress. It was *comme il faut* to attend early class unshaven and in a ragged fatigue shirt, preferably of abandoned style, from which the sergeant's or corporal's stripes had been meticulously stripped to show the shadow. Stan Seiden, a friend from "A" entry, was the master of such costuming, invariably evoking a pained matutinal look from George Boas, professor of philosophy and a Hopkins luminary of the first rank, who was in fact a veteran of *both* world wars but, well past such shenanigans, always dressed with the fastidious perfection of a French diplomat.

I blush to recall, however, that we were not above exaggerating the valor of our martial exploits. Girls were everywhere, especially abundant and eager at neighboring Goucher College, and it was not unusual, on a Saturday evening at Baltimore's German rathskeller—said to have been the prewar headquarters of the local German-American Bund—for a crowd of us to egg each other on to tales of greater and greater heroism, and thus to bigger and bigger lies, in order to impress the evening's wide-eyed dates. Whether any of them actually believed half of what she heard we did not know, but we assumed that since they manifestly were not veterans they must not realize that relatively few soldiers ever hear a shot fired at all, let alone in anger. A corollary stretcher was Joe Stefanisko's miniature Silver Star, one of the army's highest and rarest decorations for bravery, which the rest of us shamelessly borrowed, and he cheerfully lent, when the date was especially promising.

These were harmless hijinks. A more sinister note was sounded when a friend from "D" entry who'd foot-slogged his way across Europe brought his introductory German class—and, as the story spread across Home-wood, the rest of the Hopkins campus—to an awed halt. The instructor, an impeccably Prussian blond brute complete with dueling scar who was, unknown to us, an anti-Nazi refugee from the early thirties, heaped scorn on my friend's oral work, bringing his harangue to its apogee by saying, in an accent worthy of Erich Von Stroheim, "Young man, I have failed better students than you"; whereupon my friend, as if wrapping up a particularly nasty piece of house-to-house combat, rose, threw his textbook through the open fourth-floor window, said, "Yes, Herr von Glockenspiel, and I have killed better Germans than you"—and stalked out of the room.

It could be risky to cross a veteran; I knew several, even within the gentlemanly precincts of The Johns Hopkins University, who, especially after a few beers, were all too easily ignited. Some resented wounds, some imprisonment, some obscure slights or losses army service had inflicted or caused. Sudden absurdly unnecessary fistfights were uncommon but not unknown. This suggests an atmosphere of festering hostility and bellicosity that did not exist, however. Most of us were too happy to be alive and safe to want to fight anyone about anything. My guess, though it is idle to psychologize, is that we were releasing emotions the war had aroused in us for which we were not prepared. War had taken us unawares, as little more than boys still cozily lodged in the immense innocence and security of the isolated America in which we'd been born and grown up; in every theatre not only the nightmare of combat but the discovery of unanticipated human frailty, cruelty and even bestiality had piled horror upon horror, and the revulsion and fear they aroused had gone on too long, proved too exhausting. Perhaps what a later generation would tart up as "posttraumatic stress" afflicted us too (though without the benefit of counseling centers), and our sometimes exaggerated eagerness to conceal the extent to which we'd been hurt and disillusioned was a way of reentering what we devoutly hoped was "normal" life. The key word was *tough*; being *tough* became an ideal of behavior—not the toughness of the street but the toughness embodied in the movie portrayals of Humphrey Bogart, whose acrid on-screen cynicism revealed a bitter unwillingness to be deceived but did not keep him from being tender if honestly touched. Bogart and his imitators, Dick Powell and John Garfield, Robert Mitchum and Robert Ryan, and the tough-guy pictures they were making just then became touchstones; the highest praise we could give a campus friend or figure was to call him "tough-minded."

If this was an affectation the toughness of Hopkins itself was not. It was a toughness of fibre rather than style and it ran to the heart of nearly every feature of campus life. Hopkins, for one thing, was primarily a graduate institution emphasizing original research in a wide variety of academic fields—was, in fact, the first American university to be founded in emulation of the great German universities of the nineteenth century—and its serious intellectual purposes were reflected in the curriculum with which it challenged its undergraduates, a high proportion of whom would pursue graduate research and professional degrees at a time when this was still rare. Undergraduates were emphatically not neglected, as outsiders sometimes darkly hinted, and it was a matter of policy that the senior professors who were Hopkins' international glory taught at least one undergraduate course each semester; but students were encouraged at every point to remember that they were part of a larger intellectual enterprise and were expected—without coddling, tutoring or perpetual pop quizzes—to participate in it. Classes, once obligatory core courses were past, were small, intimate and Socratically demanding, and students rarely dared come to them unprepared. Nor did the Hopkins faculty play the college game. Professors on the whole were friendly and helpful but formal, did not allow personal intimacy and showed little interest in the extracurricular activities that take so much of the time and absorb so much of the energy of most college students. Hopkins supported an abundance of them—the entire range of intercollegiate and intramural sports, publications, theatre, fraternities, professional societies and dance sets—but they were the domain of the boys, not the men. The university had no "dean of students," and on the rare occasion when official disciplinary action was required the mild, agreeable dean of the Faculty of Philosophy, G. Wilson Shaffer, did what was necessary—generally, in his benign view, very little. Hopkins declined to act *in loco parentis*; campus and dormitory rules scarcely existed; students kept whatever hours they liked; class rolls were never called. Perhaps this sounds permissive, but in practice it had the intended effect of focusing undergraduate attention on what Hopkins regarded as its sole purpose: scholarship.

With no generation of students was it more successful than the generation of World War II veterans. Something of the sort happened all over the country, of course; decades later aging college professors still recalled with wistful pleasure—and perhaps with a degree of envy of their younger selves—the diligence and application of their G.I. Bill students, who remained, in memory at least, the best of their teaching careers. No doubt the legend had its oversights, for many veterans who went to college that way went on to perfectly conventional lives. Still, the atmosphere of academic seriousness was palpable and impressive, even to those of us who were part of it, and if only a fraction went on to careers of distinction the fraction was larger than American higher education had seen before or has seen since. At Hopkins the results were especially happy: the university's traditional high-mindedness, which made it forbidding for all but the most dedicated and ambitious young men, was exactly what most veterans—whose wartime experiences seemed to have purged them of the usual adolescent taste for pranks, sloth and the "gentleman's C,"—needed, sought and knew how to use.

This suggests a milieu austere, even monastic, but postwar Hopkins was nothing of the sort. For one thing, though adolescent undergraduates were a noticeable minority there were enough of them, with their cheerful innocence of real life, to brighten the darker inner lives we inevitably led; and despite our grumbling at their naivete and occasional rowdiness I suspect we were glad they were there. For another, it helped that for all its urban setting Homewood was as pastoral, with its grassy quads and abundance of trees and shrubs, as the most isolated small college in the country; and within that serenity daily life often seemed idyllic, a refuge not only from the clamor of bustling Baltimore outside but from the stresses of prolonged concentration on books and ideas and papers due next morning.

But what most helped us survive the suffocation of the academic hothouse was the simple need of us all for variety and the relief it brings. A pattern quickly set in that may have been universal among American colleges that first year after the war. The academic week, five and a half days of classes and labs, was a workweek, and we treated it as if we were factory workers trudging off to the assembly line to keep food on the family table; but the weekend was a time to howl. Howl we did too, for pleasure was still cheap and Baltimore offered it in endless abundance and variety. Eastward a few blocks from Homewood was Greenmount Avenue with its movies, restaurants, stores, bars and at least one blue-collar beer joint where draft Budweiser still went for fifteen cents a mug and where there was a perpetually renewed array of free food—pickled pig's feet, kielbasa, a huge bowl of steamed shrimp, a wheel of rat cheese; we could make an evening of it for a dollar. Downtown Baltimore, reached by a city bus that stopped every five minutes at the Charles Street corner below the dormitory, offered enough restaurants to make a man weep: Shellhase's, Miller Brothers, the House of Welch down under a railroad overpass—all of them providing Chesapeake Bay seafood so luscious it melted in the mouth—not to mention the innumerable places in this neighborhood or that serving German or Italian food for next to nothing. The House of Welch regularly offered a porterhouse steak, grilled on a plank and served that way, with a martini in front and a slice of apple pie à la mode afterward, for a buck and a quarter. Movie theatres were everywhere, including one showing French and German films none of us had seen before, and at Siegfried Weissberger's Peabody Bookshop, a block below Baltimore's Washington Monument, one might suddenly realize that the elderly man with his nose in a dusty book was H. L. Mencken, the city's indisputable sage, or Gerald W. Johnson, a famous editorialist for the *Sun*, whose imposing quarters were not far away.

Equally close by were the fleshpots of East Baltimore Street, the city's tenderloin, which specialized in more obvious indulgences: smoky gin joints, stripteasers by the dozen, a long bar, my favorite, whose length the girls paraded buck-naked, stopping here and there to encourage the solitary drinker or lonely sailor to have another and buy them one too. East Baltimore Street could be dangerous, however, for sailors were often rolled in its dark alleyways, and when we went there it was always in a crowd. A crowd, on the other hand, was rarely difficult to muster.

Such sophomoric hijinks seem tame today, when the pill and X-rated movies have robbed sex of much of the romantic mystery it held for us; but they served to relieve us of the pressures Hopkins classes sometimes imposed. We told ourselves—after a week of bookworming and paperwork—that we'd earned our Saturday nights on the town.

11

Everyone knows—and advises—that the friendship of peers is almost as valuable a part of college life as professors, courses, ideas and books; and at Hopkins I formed more than my share. Some were as transitory as the brief friendships inevitable to the perpetual movement and confusion of war; and though they occupy a pleasant corner of my memory the loss of daily campus contact led to loss of contact altogether. With others, though, I established bonds that have proved lifelong. I have no satisfactory explanation for the difference. In some friendships the basis is conscious, visible: common background, common experience, common interests, common values; but in others the foundation is unconscious, obscure, beyond reason, beyond analysis. With most of my Hopkins friends, of course, I shared the experience of war, and we came from families of comparable privilege and, on the whole, similar general ideas of what was right and wrong and what kind of society we believed worthwhile. All of us were by definition intelligent and purposeful, though the specific purposes differed widely, and all of us were committed wholeheartedly to the sort of intellectual pursuit to which Hopkins was dedicated. But in many respects we were greatly unalike. Most of my closest friends were Jews, and all but one of the lasting friendships were with Jews. All were urban, indeed metropolitan, most from New York, and spoke in the exotic accents of New York boroughs, neighborhoods, blocks. I was, by contrast, Southern, by their measure small-town and hopelessly innocent of city ways; above all I was inescapably Anglo-Saxon and Protestant, and not only Protestant but Presbyterian, argumentative often to the point of defiance. My accent amused them; they good-naturedly imitated it. Yet from the start we got along as perfectly as pups from the same litter and have gone on that way since, in unexamined trust and affection that none of us had to generate or struggle to maintain. Perhaps it was chemistry. Perhaps it was fate. I was in both senses a rebel and a Rebel: I despised rules and rulers, loved my country (North Carolina and Virginia), revered Robert E. Lee and Jeb Stuart, disbelieved Appomattox and distrusted Yankees. My friends accepted me with nods and smiles and without cavil or quibble.

This is hyperbole but contains a serious truth: though twenty-one and a grizzled veteran, as I fancied myself, I was still, inside, a raw American boy who knew himself and his country hardly at all. I did not really believe in the Confederacy, let alone worship Marse Robert, I knew only too well that the Cause was lost—as an uncle said, "When I saw Appomattox for the first time I knew why Lee surrendered"—and my own war had taught me, reinforcing my parents, that despite our differing accents I had more to learn from Yankees than they had to learn from me. Rooney Lee, who roomed with Henry Adams at Harvard in one of American history's most bizarre mismatches, was a loveable dunce but no hero of mine. I lacked what Adams deemed Lee's single strength: the "habit of command." The need to command had altogether left me somewhere in Burma. But I had not lost the need to spit authority in the eye.

The first and foremost of my Hopkins friends was an old friend, my roommate, Ira Singer, with whom I'd gone through much of the war, in Texas and India. It was he, in fact, who, half in mischief, had lured me to Hopkins after I'd made a dismissive and typically uninformed remark about it when we were in training. He was only two years my senior but often seemed at least a

generation older, for he was citified to a fault, always
impeccably dressed and in control, a tall, sleek, darkly
mysterious New Yorker who used his world-weary lan-
guor to manage his friends' lives to his satisfaction—for
which, since he was remarkably wise, benevolent and
practical, they were invariably grateful. He always knew
the best places to eat and the best dishes to order in
them, the stores for the best clothes in the best fit at the
best price, was never sick and rarely tired and at the last
desperate minute could with scarcely an instant's loss of
calm bring order and purpose to the routinely chaotic
activities of his fellow undergraduates. It followed that
despite his professions of indifference to leadership he
was our ring's inevitable leader.

It was a gift he may sometimes have cursed. My first
year at Hopkins was his last, and he was a pre-med,
taking especially demanding courses, among them genet-
ics and embryology, at a time when winning entry to any
of the nation's drastically few medical schools was com-
plicated by the huge backlog of veteran applicants. He
needed to scramble, but his prewar years at Hopkins
combined with his dependability and good judgment to
make him a natural target in Dean Shaffer's search
among returning veterans for undergraduate leaders to
help rebuild a functioning student body; and when he
tapped Ira to edit the first postwar *Hullabaloo*, the

Hopkins yearbook, which wartime shortages of students and paper had shrunk to a pamphlet, Ira could hardly decline the compliment. But almost everything of that sort—the student newspaper, the *Newsletter*; the theatre group, the Barnstormers; most intercollegiate sports— was in confusion, and persuading students to work on the *Hullabaloo*, not to mention the detailed editorial and business planning it required, would be a drain on needed study time. Almost all of us in Ira's circle signed on, but the year would tax his energies. Few pre-meds at Hopkins, I would discover before I graduated, had time for much besides their courses.

Two early friendships I made through Ira proved important to me. Arnold Ehrlich, a small, intense, sometimes sardonic man who'd been an infantryman in Europe and was in 1946 a senior, had grown up, I slowly realized, in a Philadelphia orphanage, though like most of what I learned about him I had either to deduce it or be told of it secondhand. He bore an air of mystery about him and was as intense about his privacy as he was about his interests, which were literature and philosophy. He was already a gifted and careful writer, determined to make his way in New York publishing, which he eventually did, and he had a powerful personality that could make him appealing if it did not first turn one away with its apparent indifference. He was a loner most of the time, little interested in the dormitory hubbub around him, living in a single room in "C" entry, socializing rarely, particular about whom he saw and where he went. He was usually to be found, a cigarette between his fingers and a stack of empty coffee cups at his elbow, immersed in the *New York Times* at a nearby drugstore on Charles Street, where he seemed to have a regular reservation for the little booth in the farthest corner. He was reading Carson McCullers that year, E. M. Forster and Virginia Woolf, and his interest ignited mine, for the systematic study of literature was new and exciting to me; and he talked with great spirit—and a sophistication I lacked and envied but intended to acquire at once—of Bloomsbury and the philosophy of G. E. Moore and the course he was taking in esthetics with the redoubtable George Boas, who, the father of daughters, seemed to have adopted Arnold Ehrlich as his surrogate son, a blessing I could not know would the next year, thanks to them both, become mine as well.

Kelvin Thomas was, like Ira, another of the many pre-meds around me, but otherwise he was as unlike the rest of us as it was possible to be. He was not Jewish or urban, nor even Southern; indeed he was not American or English, though had I been blind I might have mistaken his voice for Leslie Howard's. He was altogether a British citizen, born and raised in Hong Kong, and wholly

Chinese, though with a touch of American residence on his mother's side in the exotic cosmopolitan mix of his family's unusual history. In the flesh he seemed small and delicate, though he was almost as tall as I and physically strong, agile and vigorous, a fine tennis player with classic strokes and the stamina of a bull. We hit it off at once, always addressing one another as "sahib" after discovering we shared the experience of wartime India, where he'd prepared for Hopkins.

His schooling at a missionary Protestant institution in northern India had been no privileged outing, however; his risks getting there made the progress of the rest of us look staid. His father, the dean of the medical faculty at the University of Hong Kong, had named his sons after famous Victorian scientists and intended to educate them in England; but the war and the fall of Hong Kong to the Japanese had changed everything, and in its aftermath Kelvin, the youngest, had fled with an older brother into mainland China, eventually, after surviving one danger after another, fetching up in Kunming and the relative safety of westernmost Kuomintang China. There he'd somehow finagled a flight back across the Hump into India, where, amongst Protestant Britishers, he'd settled in to finish his preparatory education. Unable at war's end to return to Hong Kong, he'd taken the last money his father could raise and, at his father's instruction, embarked for Baltimore. It was the stuff of a novel, which I often urged him to write.

He and I became tennis friends, talking friends, but he seldom left campus for rowdier diversions. He studied hard, for one thing, putting in such late hours that his dorm light was often the last to go out; but for another he had no money to spare, hoarding his modest patrimony as frugally as he could against the four years ahead, working in the dining hall and dormitory office to pay some of his Hopkins expenses. Yet he said nothing of his financial difficulties and remained, when we talked, cheerful, positive, optimistic about his future in medicine, concentrating instead on the colorful family and history from which he came, always, in that gentle British accent, tolerant, measured and cool in his assessments of people and the past and the events of the day.

Events of the day, particularly political events, were a preoccupation of Hank Bobrow and Ray Carol, both of whom I'd met my astonishing first day at Hopkins. Hank, from Queens, was a bear of a man aiming at law school, and Ray, another New Yorker, planned to pursue a doctorate in political science; but what brought them closest was neither New York nor the war but an intense interest in American politics, especially Democratic politics. Like all of us—like my father and his friends from World War I—they'd returned to civilian

life determined to make the world safe from the slaughter
and desolation they had just witnessed; and if this seems
in hindsight hopelessly naive and idealistic it is also true
that it was a common faith amongst my generation of
veterans that further wars must and could be avoided by
reason and good will and the creation of institutions,
like the new United Nations, with the role and the
power to keep the peace. We were all world federalists in
spirit, if no World Federalists by affiliation, and the apparently sudden deterioration of American and British
relations with the Soviet Union, which throughout the
war we had been relentlessly urged to regard as our noble
and indispensable ally, shocked and frightened us and
made us suspect we'd been duped in more ways than one.
Hank Bobrow and Ray Carol followed the daily development of what would soon be called the Cold War with
special interest and, compared to the rest of us, expertise; and together we chewed matters to bits over more
cigarettes and more glasses of beer than were good for us.
The Republican party offered us nothing then or later,
but none of us much liked Harry Truman either, for his
feisty speeches and press conferences, so attractive in a
later time, seemed to us impulsive and unnecessarily bel-
licose. Nor could we agree on an alternative to him.
Hank and Ray inclined to Henry Wallace in 1948, but I
had a special admiration for Norman Thomas; and those

differences too got a regular—if, in my case, not very well-informed—airing. But our arguments were good-humored, for our mutual respect was high, besides which Hopkins itself was a breeding ground of ideas with an implicit faith in dispute as a way to discover truth.

None of this was as solemn as it may sound. Hank and Ray were men of immense humor, Bobrow a fount of Falstaffian good will and gusto, Carol a witty Shakespearean sideman good at observations from the corner of his mouth. But both were seniors, like so many of my first Hopkins friends, and I would see little of them after their graduation in June 1947. Others, like Len Scheer, would become closer friends in subsequent years; and still others, like Sid Offit and Reds Wolman, I had still to meet. But the year had brought me friendships for which I remain grateful. Apart from their warmth and unfailing cheerfulness, Ira and Arnold and Kelvin and Hank and Ray and all the rest, then and afterward, had brains, valued them and believed it important to use them; and what strikes me most forcibly about them, distinguishing them from most of my friends back home as well as from most of the people I know today, is the strength and richness of their inner lives. They had both intellect and imagination, and they spent much of their time in them.

The Homewood campus of Johns Hopkins, circa 1948, when it was still a pastoral setting. Gilman Hall, which housed the library and liberal-arts program, heads the central quadrangle. Homewood House, the Carroll mansion, is just to the right of the center bowl, and the single campus dorm is to its right in the lower right-hand corner of the picture.

Photograph from 1948 Hullabaloo

George Boas

Abel Wolman

Photographs from 1948 Hullabaloo

Members of the Tudor and Stuart Club, 1948.
Earl Wasserman, one of Hopkins' finest scholars, is seated right;
Charles Anderson, who all but adopted me, is third from right,
standing. I am on the far left, standing.

Photograph from 1949 Hullabaloo

Working on my Hemingway imitation my last year at Hopkins

Sid Offit

Reds Wolman

Photographs from 1949 Hullabaloo

With my sister and our parents
at the time of her graduation from Converse, 1948

Cooch

Frank Spencer, sports editor of the *Journal*.
The condition of his desk is typical.

Courtesy of the Frank Jones Photography Collection
Forsyth County Public Library
Winston-Salem, North Carolina

Nutt

Gowan Caldwell, state editor of the *Journal* and
inventor of a new language, "Nuttism."

Courtesy of the Frank Jones Photography Collection
Forsyth County Public Library
Winston-Salem, North Carolina

12

The spring term of the 1946–47 academic year was a happy time for me, not only because the war was over and I loved being at Hopkins but because the particular spirit Hopkins induced had led me to what I knew I wanted to do and be. But it was a time of drastic difficulty for one of my closest friends and of terminal disaster for another.

Ira Singer is a man of buoyant good nature, as I had discovered in the army and confirmed afterward; he takes the world as he finds it, does what he can and rarely allows himself to be frustrated by what he cannot—or over the failings of others whose gifts and tolerance are less than his. Traits like these probably are as inherent as height or the color of one's eyes, and I do not doubt that he had them as a child. In some they produce cynicism, in others an air of amused indifference; but they gave Ira a remarkable ability to absorb change and sometimes shock without apparent surprise or dismay. During his final undergraduate term his resilience was sorely tested.

He was a pre-med, of course—not uncertain of himself, as I was, but clearly committed to the long years of medical study, internship and residency ahead—and had never been anything else. As an army medic he had trained for laboratory work and ended as the ranking noncom of his hospital's laboratory in Shanghai. He had imagination as well as scientific curiosity, however, and it had led him to as broad an undergraduate curriculum as satisfying the rigorous pre-med program of the day— then heavy with advanced courses in biology and chemistry nowadays rarely required—permitted. But he had never lost sight of his goal or the requirements he must satisfy to reach it; and by his last semester he had completed an especially detailed preparation for entering medical school anywhere.

He faced an enormous obstacle, however, part circumstance, part the contrivance of others. The problem was that he was a Jew. He was neither the first nor the last Jew for whom gaining admission to a professional school, especially medical school, would be difficult; but he came to it under unusually complex circumstances in which occasion and policy coincided to deepen the problem. During the 1800s medical schools were so numerous in the United States that any male able to pay his way could get what then passed for a medical education. That access was tightened by, first, the establishment of The Johns Hopkins Medical School in 1893, which inaugurated the age of scientific medicine in America and dramatically raised the methods and standards of medical teaching; and, second, the Flexner Report of the Carnegie Foundation, which in 1910, on the basis of a comprehensive national study, called for the elevation of medical training, the creation of new criteria for accrediting medical schools and the prompt elimination of substandard programs, which were most of them. The result was that by the 1930s the number had been severely reduced—by 1947 to fewer than sixty.

Some observers critical of the American medical establishment suggested that by limiting accredited medical education to a few institutions, most of them small in student numbers, American medicine had not only raised its standards but guaranteed the financial success of its practitioners by keeping the supply small in a populous land where demand was large. Others noted that it was the common practice of medical schools to restrict the admission of Jews by imposing quotas of Jews in their entering classes. The custom was widespread and almost universally accepted but rarely acknowledged—a classic case of the "gentlemen's agreement" by which the Gentile world, especially the professional and business world, expressed an anti-Semitism that it publicly reproved in Nazi Germany and Fascist Italy.

For Ira and his generation of medical-school aspirants a further difficulty was the swollen number of applications—for relatively few places—loosed by the end of the war. Applicants who, like him, would have entered medical school in 1944 suddenly found themselves competing for admission against applicants who, but for the war, would have entered in 1943 or 1945, as well as against nonveterans who would enter, in course, in 1947. Thus what was a problem for a Jew even under normal circumstances was doubled, tripled, quadrupled or worse. He needed the best grades, the best recommendations, the best luck—or a friend on the admissions committee.

Ira's odds grew long. His grades both before and after the war were good but not Phi Beta Kappa. His recommendations would have been good enough for a WASP, but he needed better. Worse, he had no "pull" inside any medical school, and the personal warmth and good sense that ideally fitted him for medicine were almost irrelevant with competition so keen. When it became apparent that he probably would not make Johns Hopkins or

Penn I urged him to apply to Bowman Gray, in Winston-Salem, and wrote my friends there; Ira went down to be interviewed.

But it proved in vain, and in the end he failed to win admission to any of the medical schools to which he'd applied. Under ordinary conditions his record, his personal gifts and his extensive medical experience during the war would almost certainly have seen him through. But conditions were not normal, and the unusual coincidence of too many applications and Jewish quotas placed him under a handicap he was unable to surmount.

I would be vainglorious to claim that I took it harder than he—it was his future, after all, not mine—but I was deeply shocked, not only because he was my friend but because it was my first experience of anti-Semitism. As a boy I'd seen or heard neither the word nor the prejudice it stood for. My parents had Jewish friends and so had I. Jews lived down the block, on the next street, and I knew most of them. I was ignorant of their exclusion from Winston-Salem country clubs. I cannot remember hearing racial epithets before I went to V.M.I. My parents, good American liberals of their time, despised and condemned Hitler's war on the Jews. I say these things not to boast of their "tolerance"—a word they disliked because it implied the existence of something to tolerate—but to explain, most of all to myself, why I was so surprised and disappointed to discover that Americans too, and American institutions, could be guilty of the same bigotry we had fought a great war to destroy. No doubt my innocence was absurd. But it was real, and its loss hurt me and has gone on hurting ever since.

The sad story had a happy ending. Ira earned a Ph.D. in microbiology from the University of Chicago and, after holding research and teaching appointments at Rockefeller University and Georgetown Medical School, became an official of the American Medical Association, where for many years he directed the accreditation, and in several instances the establishment, of medical schools. The irony was poetic.

For Freddy Speas there would be no happy ending. Since the discovery of his leukemia in 1943 he had struggled with great determination and courage both to halt the progress of the disease and to advance normally with his studies at the Bowman Gray School of Medicine. In both he had succeeded only partially. Treatment of leukemia was still in its infancy, but thanks to his father's eminence he had been admitted to the most advanced cancer program in America, at Manhattan Memorial Hospital, where throughout the war he'd been treated successively with experimental applications of radioactive isotopes and chemicals. Brief remissions generally followed each course of treatment, only to end after weeks or at most a few months. Meanwhile, however, his movement toward his medical degree had suffered so much interruption for trips to New York that by early 1947 he had fallen behind his class by a year. Still, he'd lived longer than originally foreseen, and he remained cheerful and to all appearances optimistic about his eventual recovery; except for the single brief outburst during my early weeks home he made no reference to the gravity of his case. For most of the time he lived with other medical students in rooms near Bowman Gray. Now making daily clinical rounds at North Carolina Baptist Hospital, he'd become a familiar figure to patients and staff. He smiled a great deal.

All of that changed in the fall of 1946. He grew weaker, was often sick for days from the drugs he was taking. He moved back home—only a few blocks, but symbolic to him of his growing need for care. By Christmas he had lost his brightness of eye and quickness of step. At a Sunday dinner his parents gave for all of us who'd grown up together and spent so many years separated by the war his good humor seemed to require effort; when not talking he lapsed into an unfamiliar solemnity. His skin was the color of putty; his voice had lost its strength. Afterward, when we were all in the Speases' yard for movie-taking, he had to force his energy, to make himself walk briskly, to smile; and when I saw the film months later his enervation was so apparent I had to look away.

By early March his deterioration had made further hospital work impossible, and soon afterward, waking at home, he found he was paralyzed below the waist. I was having lunch at Hopkins when my father called to tell me Freddy was back in New York. "It looks very bad this time," he said.

I didn't wait. By early afternoon I had spoken to Dr. Bricker about cutting the day's lab in qualitative analysis and was standing on the platform at Penn Station. In New York I crossed town on foot to York Avenue and turned north. But at Manhattan Memorial they refused to let me see him till visiting hours resumed at seven, and I paced the windy blocks of the East Side in a state of agitation and apprehension, smoking cigarette after cigarette but unable to bring myself to step in, sit down and have so much as a cup of coffee. I dreaded what was happening but could think of nothing else; the glib assurances by which I'd deceived myself that Freddy would somehow "beat" his mortality now proved impossible to summon.

At last darkness fell and I was allowed upstairs. The halls smelled of death. At his door I tapped lightly and walked in. The only illumination came from a gooseneck lamp beside Freddy's bed, but from it I saw him sitting halfway upright, supported by his older brother Dixon. His disintegration since Christmas shocked me: he was dramatically thinner, his skin had no color at all and an immense lump, like the "goose eggs" we'd inflicted on each other playing football years before, protruded from his forehead. Yet through the rolling sweat of what looked like delirium he recognized me at once and launched into the story of his collapse, his paralysis and what the hospital was doing for him: a new drug, he told me again and again, nitrogen mustard, something kin chemically—he enunciated "chemically" very carefully in a high, wheezing voice—to mustard gas. Then he gave out and fell back into Dixon's arms, his eyes rolling, only suddenly to arouse himself again to my presence at the foot of the bed; whereupon, the old brightness returning, he smiled and—calling me by the name he'd given me when we were small boys together—said chirpily, "You come back soon, J. P." Gooseneck, goose egg: I went out reeling. By then I'd seen my share of dying and dead men and had come to think myself hardened; but more than forty years later I cannot expunge the memory of Freddy's dark brown eyes, huge against the whiteness of the pillow in the harsh yellow light.

I walked back across town to the small cafeteria Ira's brother and brother-in-law ran, gulped down the shot of whisky they put in my hand and drove back with them to Brooklyn, where I spent the night at Ira's mother's. Next morning I caught an early train to Baltimore, and a day later my father called again. "I'm sorry," he said.

13

By the fall of 1947 I had completed the core requirements, become a full-fledged junior and readied myself
for the upper-level undergraduate work that was, at
Johns Hopkins as elsewhere, the true proving ground of
whatever intellectual and personal qualities students intended to explore and develop. My first—sophomore—
year had been a time of indoctrination, of adjustment, of
putting out feelers this way and that; and in doing so I
had confirmed in myself a rich feeling for English poetry
and prose. To my surprise—for in my school days I'd
been thought good at algebra, geometry and trigonome-
try—I'd discovered my sense of mathematics was deficient. My interest in science had proved thin, and for
the social sciences, which did not seem to me very scientific, I was able to summon no commanding enthusiasm;

nor, though I was dogged, could I find in myself much aptitude for German or French grammar or much of an ear for even the simplest conversation. In campus life, however, I'd flourished, playing JV tennis against Annapolis, Loyola and Western Maryland; writing for the *Newsletter*; helping write and edit Ira's *Hullabaloo*; and romancing as many Goucher girls, as well as government girls in nearby Washington, as staying in good standing at a demanding college allowed. If I'd found more areas of intellectual inquiry that did not inspire me than did, well, that too, I told myself, was a valuable accomplishment. Besides, I was intensely, almost obsessively interested in literature in all its forms and tongues, not only in traditional poetry and fiction but in drama, journalism, essays, history and biography, and not only in English but in the spectrum of ancient and modern European languages—though always, alas, in translation. I wanted, moreover, to understand my fascination, to figure out not only what stirred me but why and how it did. And most of all I wanted to test my belief that I could make literature myself.

These were dreams, but dreams are a young man's business; and in any case, exacting though it often was, Hopkins was not a place to discourage dreams and dreamers, and—though by no contrivance of mine—it had designed precisely the curriculum likeliest to serve my curiosity and my ambition. To win a degree in English I must satisfy a combination of required and elective courses in the various corners of English literature; but in addition, in company with the upper-level majors in ancient and modern languages, in philosophy and in writing, speech and drama, I must complete two years in the seminars of the Literature and Language Group. These, which in total academic hours actually exceeded those I would earn in my official major, were a parallel but independent curriculum deliberately intended to offset intellectual narrowness and premature specialization.

I have experienced a great deal of good luck in my life but little to surpass, in lasting effect, the luck that Hopkins offered the literature and language seminars when it did. The program was organized in two tiers: in Classics of Literature the group read, in translation, the great ancient and modern classics of Western literature, in Classics of Thought the works of philosophy, speculation and science that have most affected and influenced human ideas. The program extended over the last two years, and each work was read under the tutelage of the reigning authority on it, on the author or on the field then resident at Hopkins. We read from the standard translations offered by the Loeb Library, Everyman's or Nelson's and were expected not only to do it thoroughly but to be ready to discuss and debate it. No quizzes were given, but on each work, as we completed it, we were required to submit a paper of three to five pages, and these were marked, graded and returned, sometimes for revision.

In practice each of the two tiers met one afternoon a week, for three hours, in the Gilman Hall seminar room of the Classics Department, a long, dusty shoebox adorned along its yellowing walls with faded steel engravings depicting antique scenes and furnished with a library table twenty feet long and chairs drawn up to it and against the walls. There, for openers, I spent three months listening to classicist Henry Rowell read and explicate Homer's *Iliad* and *Odyssey* and Virgil's *Aeneid* in the roaring manner of Lionel Barrymore berating an intern, his huge baritone booming out of his equally huge chest and leonine head, his big mouth wrapping itself with indescribable pleasure around the drama and language as he savored the surliness of Achilles and the wiliness of Ulysses, whom he called always by his Greek name, which came out a liquid and inimitable "Ody-SHOOS." Rowell's was a performance to be remembered forever, and throughout his stay he held us in thrall, enchanted tribesmen around the fire as the bard sang his song of gods and heroes and great feats and calamitous downfalls.

George Boas led us through Plato and Aristotle, his

fastidious ironies sometimes so subtle we only got them hours afterward. We read Aeschylus, Sophocles and Euripides, the Bible, Augustine and Aquinas, Machiavelli, Montaigne and Dante. Leo Spitzer, one of the world's most eminent linguists, huge, absent-minded and often nearly impossible to follow, paced the floor as he proclaimed the beauties and horrors of Rabelais; and the refugee poet and scholar Pedro Salinas parsed *Don Quixote*, which he stubbornly pronounced "Kwixott," for our enlightenment. We read Descartes, Gibbon, Goethe, Rousseau, Mill, Emerson, Darwin, Marx, Freud and William James as the two years of the sequence passed.

By the standards of many academics of the 1990s such a curriculum was not, of course, "politically correct." Its literature was wholly and unapologetically "Eurocentric," a literature, whether poetic or speculative, written by "dead white men" whose overriding aim—according to the later orthodoxy—was to maintain male domination of women, racial minorities and subject territories and peoples. It ignored the books and ideas of women. It did not acknowledge the cultures of the Middle East (apart from Hebraism), Africa and Asia. Its texts implicitly glorified masculine prowess and the military and political authority of the Atlantic and Mediterranean world. To those who had designed it, however, as well as to those then and now whose intellectual curiosity was broad enough to carry them beyond the fashions of the moment, it embraced the crucial ideas and utterances by which the world is understood, described and ordered— "the best," as Matthew Arnold proposed, "that is known and thought." Its progress summarized the evolution of mankind's dominant aims and accomplishments. It had gaps, like all curricula, but it showed us, as no mere narrative could have done, how humanity got from there to here. I shall always be grateful for its breadth, depth and elevation, and for releasing me, despite my under-graduate sloth, from the inevitable imprisonment to which living solely in the quotidian world condemns us. It could not teach me everything—no education could do that for anyone—but it opened my mind and stretched its reach as no other experience of my life, physical or cultural, has done.

Paralleling this demanding curriculum, my major courses in English proved equally absorbing. Johns Hop-kins was a notable graduate institution, had virtually introduced the modern conception of graduate research in American education and was often said, by those who did not know, to slight undergraduates as a result. The fact was that the Hopkins senior faculty routinely taught, as a matter of policy, one graduate and one undergraduate course each term, the result being that the most distinguished professors regularly held undergraduate classes and annually made the best scholarship in their fields available to undergraduates. And—an important point in light of the tendency in many places to turn detail over to graduate teaching assistants—they read and graded undergraduate papers and examinations.

No English major could manage to take everything in the English curriculum, however; so even at Hopkins, which was generous with its faculty, I could not study with everyone. I thus went where my interests led me, missing some important experiences but compensating for them with others. I had a full year of American literature, a course as sharp as any I had. I took both Shakespeare and Milton under Don Cameron Allen, doing no better than mediocre work in the former but staging a comeback in the latter, in which I won the only A in the class. My course with Earl Wasserman in the Romantic poets was definitive.

"Great men" still dominated American higher education in the 1930s and 1940s, especially in the elite colleges and universities of the East, Chicago and California, whose reputations often had been built on the names of the famous scholars they had lured to their ivied halls. The nation's educational institutions of all kinds and all degrees of quality were fewer and smaller than they soon would become, and the numbers of young Americans whose families could afford them were limited, and in this tiny world the prestige of a handful of "best" colleges frequently rested not only on their ages and histories or libraries and laboratories but on the stature of the men and women who taught in them. Johns Hopkins had been like that from its founding in 1876, making its way to the pinnacle of American education not on its venerability or association with this or that historical movement but on the eminence of its faculty.

The first and most of the second generation of the "great men" of Hopkins' early years were gone by the postwar period, but a third generation was in its vigorous prime, and at least one of the notable members of the second generation could still be seen now and then in Gilman Hall, though he was no longer active in the classroom: Arthur O. Lovejoy, famous for creating the "history of ideas" as well as author of its most influential text, *The Great Chain of Being*.

An exotic aura surrounded the rarest bird amongst Hopkins professors, W. F. Albright, universally known (behind his back) as "Foxy," which came from his middle name, Foxwell. Tall, bald, bent, with the look of an intelligent but befuddled crane, Albright might have been the model upon whom the original absent-minded professor based his image, scurrying through the corridors of Gilman Hall, his eyes huge but remote behind his round, thick glasses, as if desperate to remember what he'd forgotten. It was part of his legend that on returning to Hopkins in 1929 he'd entered a classroom at random, asked "What course is this?" and begun lecturing at once; but in fact he was one of the university's great men, the Middle Eastern archaeologist who'd virtually invented historical study of the Bible, until then mostly off-limits to critical examination within the broader contexts of history and the findings of modern archaeology. His colleagues whispered it about during my Hopkins years that he was onto "something big," and indeed he was: recognizing immediately the probable significance of the discovery of the Dead Sea Scrolls, he immersed himself in them, insisting that if they were authentic, as eventually he argued they were, they provided a Hebrew text for parts of the Bible a thousand years older than any then known. Time and the corroboration of hundreds of other scholars vindicated his views, and during the 1950s and 1960s he came to be the world's leading authority, his knowledge and experience sought everywhere. To the undergraduates of my generation, however, he was a uniquely "Hopkinsian" character, an occasional lecturer and campus landmark whose appearance and air of utter bewilderment might have come from the pages of Dickens. "Foxy" he may well have been in personality as well as nickname: the constant confusion he projected helped gain him time and distance in which to concentrate on his immense and invaluable work.

Another oddity was the elongated clown of the Department of History, Sidney Painter, who was its chairman as well as a scholar of international renown in his specialty, English history. He was easily the tallest man on campus, probably as close to seven feet as to six, and he moved through the corridors of Gilman Hall with the wary deliberation of a large, caged animal—perhaps the cat produced by some grotesque mutation—trying not to damage the doorways or passersby. He had a mane of coal-black hair, a lock of which had generally slipped across his forehead by midmorning, and a bushy black mustache to match; and to round out things his pipe only left his mouth to permit his lewd, rasping chuckles, which frequently could be heard from one end of the building to the other. He had a fund of bawdy stories from which he constantly drew, chortling and choking as he struggled through clouds of smoke to tell them for the hundredth or thousandth time. He loved to shock and delight undergraduates with lectures abounding in anecdotes about chastity belts, the difficulty of shedding medieval armor for sexual intercourse and the facilities to accommodate excretion at the Tower of London; but outside Hopkins he was known for his scholarship, which had produced numerous books and papers.

Almost as familiar a campus figure was Owen Lattimore, the renowned Sinologist, whom we saw most mornings pacing the brick terrace before Gilman Hall talking earnestly with a brightly costumed lama, wrongly believed by us to be the Dalai Lama, who was then, thanks to Lattimore, in residence at Hopkins. We would hear more of Lattimore, in another context, a year or two later.

Abel Wolman, a senior professor of engineering, was an important man in the great world too. The youngest of three gifted brothers—the others a professor at the Johns Hopkins School of Medicine and a professor of economics at Columbia—he was a pioneer in water and sanitation whose engineering skills were sought everywhere; he devised systems not only for the large cities of the United States and Europe but for the entire country of Israel. To most students, however, he was simply the most popular figure at Hopkins, friendly, funny and the best after-dinner speaker any of us ever heard. Angular and spare, with fine white hair and a long nose, he had a house just off campus, on Charles Street, where, as a friend of his only child, "Reds," I went often to dinner; and it was at dinner there, deep in the animated conversation Abel Wolman seemed to generate, that I first heard—from him, of course—the word *ecology*.

None of these Hopkins monuments was especially

"Chipsian." Though in some instances their idiosyncrasies fitted stereotypes of the eccentric professor—absentmindedness, long hair before it became fashionable, careless dress—they did not coddle undergraduates, were said to make severe demands of their graduate students and did not dispense tea and sympathy; though friendly and invariably helpful in clarifying intellectual confusion they maintained an impersonal relationship with students, treating them not like bewildered adolescents but like fellow toilers in the common task of learning. Serious themselves, they affected to assume that their charges were serious too, as indeed most, given that encouragement, became. The casual intimacy between faculty and undergraduates I encountered when a few years later I became a teacher at a small Southern college would have seemed foreign, and inappropriate, at Hopkins.

14

If playing warm, cuddly Mr. Chips would have been frowned on at Hopkins, however, close friendships between professors and undergraduates were not unknown; and with two senior faculty members I established closer—even familial—ties, in both cases feeling by the time I graduated that I had become virtually an adoptive son.

George Boas was by my time a leading Hopkins figure, not only revered as lecturer, writer and co-founder of the History of Ideas Club but as campus wit and conscience, as a social activist who could be counted on to stand up, bravely and often alone, for high principles of intellectual honesty and human rights. The prime case was Hopkins Professor Owen Lattimore, who taught international relations and who, famous worldwide as both Orientalist and political analyst, became one of the first victims of McCarthyism, pilloried for helping America "lose" China. Boas led a movement at Hopkins to support Lattimore, and the support helped to restore Lattimore's reputation and to discredit McCarthy's.

I did not enter Boas's orbit by any such avenue, alas, though I had courses under him; my friendship with him came from my lonely friend of 1946–47, Arnold Ehrlich, who upon graduation had bequeathed me to Boas, urging him to take me, as he had taken Arnold, under his avuncular wing. This Boas did almost at once. When I returned in the fall for my junior year I found a note from him in my Gilman Hall box saying he hoped I would come for dinner Sunday at his farm in Baldwin, outside Baltimore, and would have me picked up at noon. We had never met, in fact, and my heart was in my throat; but I accepted by return note and was thus launched on what proved one of the most precious associations of my life.

Boas was hardly a paradox, but to the casual eye much about him seemed contradictory. His look—he was small, dark, dapper and bald, with a precise mustache— was that of a French intellectual or diplomat, and his manner, elegant and witty, supported the impression; but he was deeply American, a native of Rhode Island, educated there and at Berkeley, a veteran of two world wars, devoted husband and father of two daughters and the working owner of a handsome Maryland farm, on which he raised horses and behaved like an honest countryman rather than a boulevardier. His wife, Simone, a noted French sculptress whose magisterial presence perfectly offset his restless air of the cosmopolitan gadfly, dispensed hospitality and calm at a table where the food was legendary.

They put me instantly at ease, plying me with martinis, chicken, wine and rapid-fire conversation punctuated by George's wisecracks and guffaws. Their daughter Kittsy was there with her husband, my Hopkins classmate Bill Dinsmore—it was they who'd driven me to the farm—and some others I've since forgotten; the Dinsmores, my age, helped me past my initial awkwardness. It was across the table that afternoon that I discovered George and I had another, if slight, connection beyond Hopkins and Arnold Ehrlich. During World War II he had served the navy as an art expert, driving all over France and the Low Countries recovering and authenticating artwork of which Hitler and his goons had looted Europe, but in the first war he had been an army officer and aide to Major General Charles E. Kilbourne, superintendent of V.M.I. when I was a cadet; Kilbourne had made a son of him, as George would make a son of me. Their families were close, and George made regular trips to Lexington, Virginia, where the old soldier was living in retirement, to keep the friendship alive. I could not foresee, of course, that in a few years I too would be living only a few blocks from the general or that George would soon combine visits to Kilbourne with stays at my house.

Still less could I foresee how profoundly, at Hopkins and afterward, George Boas would influence my life. Though in the classroom I found him lively and stimulating I was not a student of philosophy in any scholarly sense, nor was it as a pedagogue at a lectern that he affected me; it was through his fascinating company and conversation that he "taught" me most. What he taught me is not so easy to say: an attitude perhaps, a style of thought, a way of asking good questions. His own questions were the key. He always insisted that the terms of discussion be clear and precise; he constantly demanded greater refinement of language. The range of his curiosity was extraordinary: ideas had origins, connections, implications, and they generally grew beyond the artificial bounds of any particular discipline. He wanted to know—though he knew all knowledge was incomplete—about everything: politics, science, literary figures and trends, what generations younger than his own were thinking and doing, who painted what and what it meant. Though probably the most serious man I would ever know he was also one of the funniest, given to puns, to a love of ironies, coincidences and oddities, to comic improvisations foretelling the inevitable consequences of this action or that. Yet his human sympathies were deep, and he never stopped to assess the cost of befriending— or defending—an embattled colleague, as he would do for Owen Lattimore. Like all great teachers, I suspect, he mostly taught himself. To know him was to know a pinwheel of ideas and stories; but when the excitement faded it became apparent that the ideas were crucial and that the stories had points.

My other surrogate father from the Hopkins faculty, Charles Anderson, was as unlike Boas as it was possible to be, though they were friends and, in later life, neighbors. Anderson was a Georgian and in his earlier years had studied law, and his look and manner, in contrast to the Gallic cosmopolitanism that was so striking in Boas, were those of a Southern aristocrat, which—though the mannerisms seemed unconscious—is what he was. He too was of only medium height, but he boasted a more powerful build; he had a thick mop of gray hair and a profile so chiseled he might have posed for one of the Arrow Shirt advertisements of the twenties. He was no languid antebellum lounger, however; his scholarship had produced a major study, *Melville in the South Seas*, a professorship at Duke and, by the time our paths crossed, the prestigious appointment as Caroline Donovan Professor of English at Hopkins.

I had no prior access to him through the good offices of Arnold Ehrlich, who did not, in fact, especially like him; but my questions—and my answers to his famous classroom cross-examinations—provoked his curiosity during my junior-year course with him in American literature, in which it soon became apparent that I shared his interest in Stephen Crane, Frank Norris and, above all, Henry James. He encouraged me to write papers on them, and then, as the year and the course neared their ends, he urged me to go ahead and do the long paper I wanted to do on F. Scott Fitzgerald. This was a minor unorthodoxy at Hopkins, which still frowned on the study of contemporary writing, believing it too new to have definitive status; and it was particularly chancy with Fitzgerald, for he had been dead only a few years, his *oeuvre* was small, all of his books were out of print and critics disagreed drastically about their worth. But Anderson ignored such objections, egged me on, reread all of Fitzgerald's books himself and even approved when I told him I wanted to write Arthur Mizener, at Carleton College, who was writing what in a few years would prove to be the first in a torrent of Fitzgerald biographies. I did—eventually having breakfast with Mizener when he came through Baltimore on a research trip—and the entire experience, which all but consumed the spring term, sealed our friendship.

It was not, to be sure, the friendship of equals, for he was the priest and I the acolyte; but it was clearly enduring and would change as the years passed. To some who knew him befriending me seemed out of character: they thought Anderson stuffy, a latter-day Dixie bourbon and probably a snob; but I soon discovered, on increasingly frequent visits with him and his wife, Eugenia, that like me he was a rebel who hid his independence and iconoclasm behind an exterior of conventional dress and behavior. What made our mutual affections was easy to see: we were both committed sons of the Old South who fretted not only at the New but at the South's traditional somnolence and indifference; our personalities were much alike, for both of us were quick, impatient, irritated by sloppy thinking and language; and, in his mid-forties, he badly needed the son he lacked and now knew he and Jeanie would never have. But we did not have to spell out our affinities; they were simply there, as they are in most friendships, and at Hopkins and in the decades to come he was content to play the doting father to my restive but promising son.

15

It was during my last two years at Hopkins that I began to realize how much easier it was to want to be a writer than it was actually to write. My decision to abandon further pre-medical studies and to work instead toward a career in writing had been almost as big a surprise to me as it was to my parents and friends; but I had made it in good faith and with more self-confidence than it probably deserved, and I never looked back afterward in belated doubt or with regret. It was knowing how to do what I proposed to do that was difficult.

I had always written, to be sure, and written easily as well as to the satisfaction of my mentors and editors. But brief and longer term papers, mostly to themes set by others, or newspaper sports stories whose subjects were given, whose limits in time and place were fixed and whose resolutions were clear, were one thing; making it up and developing what resulted were another altogether. There were no rules. Neither ideas nor forms were there for the taking. There was, in fact, no right or wrong.

All novice writers make this discovery, of course, and all are initially dismayed by it. I made another not all novices share: the discovery that—though I was naturally articulate, even facile, and absorbed the diction and rhythms of English easily—I had no great talent for invention. Stories and plots did not simply pop into my head. I had a profound interest in human character and more curiosity about it than may have been wise; but imagining the narrative vehicles by which character could be dramatized proved far more demanding, and usually the ones I managed to invent were thin and artificial. I went on trying and saved what I wrote, but it became unambiguously clear to me that I not only had much to learn but would have to learn it on my own.

This is another way of saying that I did not expect anyone to teach me to write in the way studio masters teach students to play the piano or cello or to use paintbrush or chisel. I was not interested in the courses or major offered by the new Department of Speech, Writing and Drama, though I liked and respected the poet Elliott Coleman, its founder and chairman, whose kindness and generosity to young writers had already made him the nurturing spirit of writing ambitions at Hopkins. (The department became nationally known a few years later when it was changed to The Writing Seminars, a solely graduate program.) My belief was that for me the best avenue toward writing my own books was to read the great books of the past and to master them if I could; the writing department's focus on Modernism, in particular Joyce, Proust and Eliot, seemed to me unnecessarily narrow and limiting; I wanted to read *everything*.

That I could not read everything, no matter how long I lived and how hard I tried, was another distressing discovery, even if every young writer before me had made it; and in any event I did my best in my English courses and in the reading program of the Language and Literature Group. I read widely on my own as well, besotted by Fitzgerald and Hemingway, who seemed almost my contemporaries; elevated by Henry James, whose beautifully constructed late novels richly satisfied my obsession with order and shape and whose sonorous labyrinths of language seemed transcendently lovely and mysterious; lured as if hypnotized into the England of Virginia Woolf and E. M. Forster. But I admired equally the prose of Browne, Dryden, Gibbon, Henry Adams and Max Beerbohm, to name only a few; and if I have a criticism of the way English was taught in the late 1940s, not only at Hopkins but almost everywhere, it is that its emphasis on fiction and poetry, and overwhelmingly on long fiction, left in me the conviction that other prose forms—the essay, history, biography, journalism—were insignificant genres alongside The Novel. No one ever said that outright; but like many of my generation I came away believing that unless I wrote novels, and masterpieces at that, I had subtly but surely seated myself below the salt.

The novel was the ruling literary form of the day, in any case, and the stress English studies placed on it may only have echoed what was already in the air. In my innocence—not yet knowing how difficult writing was—I had written one myself, soon blessedly lost, while in India. Popular magazines like *Life* and *Time* regularly asked who would be the next generation of American novelists. Half the literary students I knew at Hopkins claimed to have novels in progress. The previous generation—Fitzgerald, Hemingway, Faulkner, Dos Passos, Wolfe, Wilder—had been spectacular, and it seemed inevitable that critics should wonder who their successors would be. New books from Richard Lockridge, Jean Stafford, Calder Willingham, Thomas Heggen and Truman Capote aroused widespread enthusiasm, and—as if my generation were yearlings entered against thoroughbreds—the overriding question became who would chal-

lenge Hemingway (or Cummings or Dos Passos or Re-
marque) by writing the great novel of World War II.
Presently we got *The Young Lions* and *The Naked and the
Dead* and the race was on, with dozens of less publicized
entries, many excellent, drawn from the wartime experiences of their authors. For young writers fresh from the
fighting fronts of the world it was the thing to do, and those
of us who had still to do it fretted to start.

Few of us even knew how to do that; but fortunately
the atmosphere at Hopkins encouraged our dreams. The
cafeteria at Levering Hall, where everyone gathered for
coffee and conversation, always had a long table around
which aspiring campus writers heatedly argued through
huge clouds of cigarette and pipe smoke, sometimes as
many as a dozen conflicting opinions at once. It was at
one such session that Bill Wishmeyer, an older undergraduate of formidable intelligence and erudition, began
talking learnedly about some forgotten masterpiece for
the benefit of Mike Adamovich, who invariably had
read whatever anyone else talked about and had a firmer
grasp of it to boot. The rest of us nodded stuporously,
never having so much as heard of the lost monument,
but soon Adamovich was busy finding subtle truths and
implications in this aspect or that—only to be told,
before God and us all, that Wishmeyer had invented the
whole thing, that the "masterpiece" did not exist and

that Adamovich was simply full of hot air. Crimson with embarrassment and rage, he beat a humiliated retreat and did not turn up again for a week.

Just around the corner, but still on Levering's lower level, was another literary hangout: the offices of the two undergraduate publications, the weekly *Newsletter*, an eight-page newspaper, and *Hullabaloo*, the yearbook. Ira Singer's editorship of the 1947 annual had drawn me into it, first as associate editor of the 1948 book, then as editor in chief my senior year; but many of the same people worked for both, and traffic was brisk between the two scruffy offices, whose sole merit was that they boasted a pair of battered typewriters that looked like relics of Mark Twain's famous experiments. *Newsletter* staffers actually did most of their writing and editing in the *Newsletter* office, where the most raffish Hopkins students usually could be found if not drinking coffee next door; but neither I nor any of the editorial or business staffs of *Hullabaloo* used our office for anything but a convenience. I laid out *Hullabaloo* pages, cropped pictures and wrote copy in my dorm room, and the business manager and his minions sold ads out of their coat pockets. I used the Levering Hall room for bull sessions and occasionally—on weekends or campus-dance evenings—for assignations with Goucher girls and student nurses from Union Memorial. The *Newsletter* crowd across the hall generally spilled over into our space on deadline nights, borrowing our typewriter and long worktable. Writing for the two publications—and the *Blue Jay*, a raucous humor magazine that came along in 1949 to launch the career of Bill Clinger, a future Republican congressman from Pennsylvania—seemed a natural part of the Hopkins literary whirl, in any case; and sooner or later, either for me or for Sid Offit, the genial *Newsletter* editor, everyone who had the faintest interest in writing found himself cranking out cutlines or movie reviews or profiles of student leaders and other riffraff or covering a sports event or a symposium to which no one else had been assigned. I wrote a weekly *Newsletter* column, "Knee Deep," which regularly provoked the question, "Knee deep in what?"; Sid hacked copy for me; and a future *New York Times* columnist and Pulitzer Prize winner, 1947 editor Russ Baker, and his dyspeptic sidekick, Bill Gresham, collaborated on a play, *The Whites of Their Eyes*, at whose climax the battleship *Missouri* majestically steamed up Charles Street, all guns trained on Hopkins.

The company was equally agreeable, though more subdued, at the Tudor and Stuart Club, where I spent a lot of time too. Sir William Osler, one of the four "Great Doctors" immortalized by John Singer Sargent for their pioneering roles during the founding days of The Johns

Hopkins Hospital and School of Medicine, had established and endowed the club in memory of his son Revere, killed during World War I, and it occupied—uniquely at Hopkins—a private, paneled clubroom on the top floor of Gilman, to which members, given keys, had access at all hours. The clubroom had a fireplace and, behind one set of panels, a small butler's pantry stocked with tea and coffee and china and cutlery. Glass-fronted cases lined the inside wall, filled with Revere Osler's rare books, and the wall above the mantel held his portrait, beside which stood his angling gear. A fine long library table surrounded by comfortable study chairs occupied the center of the room but left enough space, around the walls, for big leather easy chairs, in one or another of which some hungover graduate student or ancient professor usually could be found dozing. The Osler endowment had specified that the senior membership should be evenly split between Homewood liberal-arts and medical-school faculty from across town; and a handful of memberships was offered to graduate students in English, classics and history and to upper-level undergraduates. The club's secretary—actually its dog robber—was by tradition one of the latter, and in my senior year the duty fell to me.

The duty was scarcely arduous. I saw to it that supplies of tea and coffee were maintained and that the pewter humidor on the mantel was always filled with expensive pipe tobacco, which the graduate students routinely used to fill not only their pipes but their pouches; I kept the petty cash in a locked cupboard, and once a month I sent out postcards inviting all members *in facultate* and *in urbe* to a Friday-evening smoker in the clubroom, then ordered the sandwiches and beer that were the customary fare. Someone else arranged for speakers, who seated themselves, properly beered and sandwiched, beside the fire; and among the most memorable of them were Stephen Spender, seeming very like Shelley with his long hair and flowing silk tie, and Robert Frost, already a poetic Mount Rushmore, complaining again and again, this being in the earliest days of Pound's incarceration a few miles away in Washington, about "Ezra's foolishness, his confounded foolishness." I also received a monthly postcard of regret from H. L. Mencken, Baltimore's most famous figure, who had recently suffered a tragic stroke; the cards, signed for him by Mrs. Rosalie Lohrfinck, his devoted secretary, were fastidiously polite. Both cozy and exclusive, the Tudor and Stuart Club—"T and S" to members—served me nobly as a campus bolt hole, a place quieter and more comfortable than the crowded university library in which to read and write or gab on into the night with others interested in books and writing; and among its treasures was an immense collection of indecent limericks, to which I am proud to say I contributed a few unaccountably missing until then.

Though activities like student publications and the Tudor and Stuart Club were wholly extracurricular they helped sustain my literary ambitions, for they made it clear, as formal courses could not, that writing and publishing were not merely something done in the past, by men and women now dead, but were as alive and contemporary as the morning newspaper or the latest Broadway hit. The postwar years were, in fact, a boom time not only for an entire new generation of novelists and poets but for new American playwrights, who were exciting to read about and whose brilliant new plays were giving the American stage a whole new life. My walls were covered with pictures, clipped from the *New York Times* and *PM*, of Tennessee Williams, Arthur Miller and Thomas Heggen and scenes from their plays; and many of us got to see some of the best before they opened on Broadway. Baltimore was still one of the two or three favorite tryout towns, and Ford's Theatre one of the favorite sites, to make final cuts and rearrangements before going into New York with a new production; Ford's invariably offered last-minute unsold seats for a dollar. It was thus that I saw, among many others, *Mister Roberts*, *South Pacific* and *Command Decision*. And though I missed *A Streetcar Named Desire* and *Death of a Salesman*, which tried out elsewhere, it was nothing to catch a train for New York to see them, for both fares and tickets were cheap and the ride short, or to make a weekend of it with Hopkins friend Bob Zadek's family in suburban Westchester; at his stepmother's instruction we allowed ourselves to be driven into town for a Saturday matinee of the Robinson Jeffers translation of Euripides' *Medea*, of which Judith Anderson was making a spectacular success, ably and even self-effacingly assisted by John Gielgud, of whom till then I'd only read. I came out of the theatre into the cold evening air vowing to consecrate my life to the theatre, to make myself the toast of New York, London and the civilized world. This mania lasted no further than Baltimore, but the memory of Judith Anderson, her presence like seeing lightning strike, proved to be enduring.

Nothing did more to confirm me in my choice of a vocation, however, than being a member of the little circle of would-be writers around Tommy Chastain, into whose benevolent graces Arnold Ehrlich had also bequeathed me. Chastain had no real connection with Hopkins beyond a night course or two and the friends he made there, and he was already busily employed in writing advertising copy for one of the numerous Baltimore radio stations; but he had an overriding ambition to write novels and live in New York, which for him and many another still stood as the golden symbol of American writing and publishing, and he worked tirelessly toward both ends. Some accident of birth or circumstance had left him partly handicapped, but his mind and spirit remained invincibly bright. From time to time, in response to a card or phone call, I gathered with others for an evening of beer and talk at his mother's house on Twenty-fifth Street, a short walk from Hopkins.

Tommy's studio was on the top floor, the third floor, a couple of small rooms, reached by a dim staircase, where he had his desk and typewriter and books; the walls were adorned with framed photographs of his favorite writers—Steinbeck, Cain, Hammett, Chandler—and the proverbial plastering of rejection slips from every major and minor magazine in America. I no longer remember the names of the others, for few had been to Hopkins, but the center of everything was Tommy Chastain himself, generously doling out beer and sandwiches and insisting on knowing what we all had read and written since our last time there. We shared an enthusiasm for tough-guy detective stories and movies, and Tommy even wanted to write his own, which he eventually did with great success; and many of us were interested as well in radio drama, then enjoying its last great popularity. Tommy, in fact, had only recently sold a radio dramatization of Walter Van Tilburg Clark's *The Ox-Bow Incident* to one of the weekly radio theatres, which planned it as a vehicle for the actor Van Heflin—though at the last minute the objections of several Southern affiliates to a story depicting a lynch mob "unfavorably" (it was not clear how a lynch mob could be depicted favorably) caused the sponsors to cancel the show.

No one at Tommy's except the two of us went on to writing careers, and little was said that proved consequential or illuminating or even especially wise; but an atmosphere of mutual interest and encouragement is indispensable for a young writer, who often fears that what he is trying to do will be not only inadequate but of interest to no one but himself. Tommy Chastain's unpretentious little evenings high atop a narrow Baltimore row house were for me the thing I needed most at the time I needed it most, the equivalent of a fine Paris salon to which I'd at last been invited and in which my gifts and promise had at last been recognized.

16

Charles Anderson wanted me to return to Hopkins as a graduate student, eventually to earn a Ph.D. in English and go into college teaching and scholarship. Earl Wasserman urged me to consider it carefully, and Don Cameron Allen supported him. I was immensely flattered, for in those days only a chosen few got such encouragement, and I was deeply attracted to academic life and what I took to be its serenity and freedom from the bustle outside; but by the midpoint of my senior year I had decided against it and chosen to move in another direction.

Young people often feel torn by conflicting impulses, which arise from the diversity of opportunities available to them; this was abundantly true in the years immediately following World War II, when the United States, emboldened by its success not only in waging and win-ning the greatest armed conflict in history but also in developing the industrial resources to support it, confi-dently and enthusiastically expanded itself in every di-rection. My temptation to enter graduate studies was deepened by Anderson's offer to get me a fellowship that would make it possible. The apparent ease with which scholarship was conducted and the apparent leisure of its practitioners were an additional lure. Yet at some point it became clear in the fall of 1948 that they were not for me.

Knowing one's strengths and limitations is the key to making such decisions, however, and I cannot claim that I had more than an intuitive understanding of myself; but a few traits in my personality offered warnings. My impatience, for one, seemed to fit me poorly for the schol-ar's need to move deliberately, even slowly, through re-search materials, to weigh patiently, to postpone judg-ment until details are complete. I had been a good student at Hopkins, attentive and punctual; but my success de-pended, I realized, on conscientious preparation, quick-wittedness and a glib pen. I was too restless to bury myself in the library stacks, as some did, or to spend a weekend in preparing multiple drafts of an important paper, as others could; I was too interested in sports, girls and the pleasures of the senses. Though I often saturated myself in books and writers whose work I liked the absorption ended when I'd learned what I wanted to know and could move on to the next passion. Above all, however, I detested the necessity to specialize, to spend more and more time on less and less; rightly or wrongly I was a generalist, perhaps a dilettante, and I knew without spelling it out that the high scholarship I so admired in Anderson and Wasserman and Allen and Boas required aptitudes I could not boast.

Another consideration—though I did not discuss it with my mentors—was that in my mid-twenties I was simply tired of school. It was not a complaint against Hopkins but an expression of my natural restlessness that I felt I had prepared for life long enough and now needed to live it. By then, moreover, I'd done almost everything an undergraduate could do at Hopkins except play lacrosse: I was editor of *Hullabaloo* and wrote a weekly column for the *Newsletter*; I'd played JV tennis and intramural football and softball; I'd made Tudor and Stuart and Omicron Delta Kappa, both honors, and founded the first Hopkins Film Society; I'd attended enough dance sets at the Alcazar in downtown Baltimore to satisfy my social needs for years to come and costarred in the Barnstormers production of *The Front Page*, chewing up the scenery as that scoundrel of an editor, Walter Burns. I'd even, with Hopkins' blessing, gone for a

Rhodes Scholarship, losing deservedly to a West Point cadet and a fine student at St. John's. I was not so much tired of it all as ready for something else.

The worst about leaving would be leaving friends. During my last two years I'd established several friendships that would prove as enduring as those with Ira Singer and Tom Chastain. The first was with Sid Levin, the explosive *Hullabaloo* editor in chief between Ira and me, a Baltimorean and veteran whose high energy and goofy good humor were matched by a contentiousness as hair-trigger as my own. We were together constantly my junior year putting together the 1948 book and automatically went on to friendship that was both social and political. He was an ardent liberal in the New Deal tradition, dubious about Harry Truman and apprehensive about the emerging Cold War, which he and many of our generation regarded as a contradiction of everything we'd lost so many years to achieve. I could agree with him on that but not on his fervent support of Henry Wallace and the Progressive party in what was becoming a four-way presidential race in 1948. We disagreed amicably—I had determined to cast my first presidential vote for Norman Thomas, who wasn't even on the ballot in North Carolina—but our friendship almost foundered when Hopkins President Isaiah Bowman, a Hoover-collar conservative, refused to let Wallace speak on campus. Wallace managed to give his speech a few feet off-campus to a huge student audience sitting on-campus, and Sid decided angrily to punish Bowman, who was retiring that year, by withdrawing the yearbook dedication to him. I hated what Bowman had done too but believed the dedication was obligatory, and Sid and I shouted and screamed at each other for days, finally compromising on an ambiguous dedication to "One World" on one page and a big picture and tribute to Bowman, which I wrote, on the next. We could not quarrel forever, fortunately—Sid looked like a Jewish leprechaun and recovered his temper as quickly as he lost it; and it did not hurt that by then he was engaged to Esther Rubinstein, a Baltimore girl we all liked who was too bright to endure a breach of friendship over something as trivial as the dedication of an undergraduate annual.

Len Scheer was as innocent of contentiousness as Sid Levin and I were guilty; in what is now nearing fifty years of friendship I have never known him to quarrel with anyone. Almost swarthily dark and as lithe as a bamboo cane, he graced our crowd at Hopkins with a serene good nature that perpetually twinkling eyes and a beatific smile only enhanced. He was scarcely a saint, however, for his way with girls quickly made him a campus legend: a quick compliment and a flash of teeth and they melted on the spot. John Dower, a dormitory friend, always referred to him, in awe, as "the little bastard," but in fact his chivalry was so winning that his numerous girlfriends invariably went on adoring him long after they'd gone their separate ways, calling him for advice at odd hours and suggesting, before the conversation ended, "If you ever . . ." He was a veteran of the war in Europe, a cross-country runner of renown, the friend whose balance and good sense the wise amongst us sought in a jam; but what he was studying at Hopkins remains as mysterious to me today as it was then. Compared to girls it seemed not to matter.

Sid Offit, on the other hand, was as emotional and as effusive as Len was calm and controlled. Another Baltimorean, he lived with his parents and younger brother nearby and walked back and forth daily, though unlike many local students he led a busy campus and extracurricular life. We'd met through tennis when paired for doubles against Annapolis but became close friends only during my last year, when he was editor of the *Newsletter* and we discovered we both dreamed woozily of becoming "real" writers. He was a few years younger than most of us but unfazed by our swagger; instead of quaking before our bluster he had the disarming habit of asking leading questions: "So did you ever see Mountbatten?" or "What is it like to be shot at?" Above all, however, he was drunk on books, gulping them down and begging for more, demanding advice on which courses to take and what professors had something to say. He was quick, excitable, always in motion, and like many who have such energy he sometimes seemed harum-scarum; but he had a remarkable, almost animal warmth, a gift for affection upon which his friends quickly came to depend.

No one who ever saw him had to ask why M. Gordon Wolman was called "Reds." His hair was so red it shone across a lacrosse field, where he shone himself, and he had the bright, freckled face to match it. He too was a Baltimorean, but with the important distinction that he was a campus brat, the son of engineering Professor Abel Wolman, Homewood's most popular figure. He lived just off campus and literally had only to cross Charles Street to go to class. No doubt the popularity of his father would have carried him a long way anyway, but Reds was himself a boy of extraordinary appeal, a fine student, nationally respected lacrosse player and, as chairman of the Student Activities Committee, effectively president of the Hopkins student body. I no longer remember how it happened that we became such close friends, for our interests ran in different directions and we had no classes together; but I liked him, as everyone did, and near the beginning of my senior year he began stopping by my dorm room on his way home to see if I wanted to catch a movie later, and soon he was asking me to dinner with his parents. The Wolmans' house was turned sideways to fit its narrow city lot, the first I'd ever seen like that; the "front" door actually was on the side. The dining room and kitchen occupied the ground floor, in the European fashion, another first for me, with the large, book-lined living room up a flight, its street side an immense bow window that might have come, like the whole house, from London. Reds had the entire top floor to himself, a sitting room, bedroom and bath; and after the most entertaining dinners I had ever attended, his father and mother prodding both of us with questions and jokes, he and I tramped upstairs to talk the evening away. He aimed at an academic career of his own, was already accepted for graduate study in geology at Harvard for the fall of 1949, and it was from him, an undergraduate majoring in geography, that I got my first lessons in the new field—or amalgam of fields—of environmental study and engineering. He was not his father's child for nothing and a few years later returned to Hopkins as a professor in his own right, launching an interdisciplinary program in environmental studies that would make him a pioneer figure in what would become a crucial area of modern life. All that was fascinating enough, but what I valued even more highly was his remarkable vitality, which expressed itself in both vigorous physical grace and humor that, like his father's, was simultaneously witty and commonsensical.

I would miss the lively company of Hopkins faculty

and friends and much else besides: listening to T. S. Eliot read his poetry at the National Gallery in Washington, tall, stooped, funereal, the utter antithesis of the romantic stereotype of a revolutionary artist; Baltimore's easy Europeanism, its squares and bowered streets, its pleasure in food and drink, its respect for art and music and theatre, its cosmopolitan ambience, part German, part English, part Jewish, with an unmistakable dash of the antebellum South for thickening; the abundance of nearby women's colleges and girls; the primacy of lacrosse, which had brought Hopkins national championships all three of my years there and made Baltimore the only city in the land where it was routine to see small boys playing catch after school with sawed-off attack sticks instead of baseballs and fielders' gloves; Maryland crab cakes and soft-shell crabs fresh from the Chesapeake Bay, and cheap Arrow Beer, brewed in Baltimore . . .

But it was time to go. I had been a schoolboy long enough and did not want to be the sort of student who finds excuses for staying on year after year. Besides, I had a more positive reason to welcome graduation in June 1949. I had a challenge I greatly looked forward to meeting: my first real job.

17

Climbing the stairs to the second-floor newsroom of the *Winston-Salem Journal & Sentinel* I was overwhelmed suddenly with the feeling, rare in any life, that I was doing exactly the right thing. The stairs creaked, the building was rank with the smell of printer's ink and the walls shook as the presses in the basement launched the final edition of the afternoon paper. It was a minute or so till two on a hot June Saturday in 1949. I had graduated from Johns Hopkins on Tuesday and driven to North Carolina on Wednesday, and now I was coming to work—real work, a real job—for the first time.

I was twenty-four and by any measure late to start, but four years of war and three of college had delayed me. It was thus an occasion to go to work at last; and if I make a point of calling it a "real" job it is simply because until then I'd never had one. I had not been hopelessly idle. In high school I'd had a paper route and I'd worked, when called, as a sports-page stringer. I'd spent three summers as a laboratory helper at the Bowman Gray School of Medicine and a fourth trapping and freezing ordinary houseflies from selected backyards of Winston-Salem, Greensboro and High Point for a nationwide epidemiological study of the Yale Medical School. I had worked hard at all of them, but mostly for pocket money, mostly courtesy of research grants and in no case as a regular, permanent employee. I'd been a kid and I'd had kid jobs. But working full-time as a newspaper report-er—that was, in the old American expression, the gen-uine article. As H. L. Mencken said of the same moment in his own life, I had cause to envy no man.

I was luckier than I knew. By 1949 mergers and con-solidations had reduced the number of American dai-lies—and available jobs—to a twentieth-century low, which the abundance of returning veterans and the con-tinued proliferation of journalism-school graduates did nothing to ease. In my innocence, knowing nothing of the reality of the field I proposed to enter, I'd blandly taken it for granted that any newspaper must automat-ically be panting for my arrival. In fact, however, I owed my job less to my own brilliance than to the fortunate coincidence that my mother had run into W. K. Hoyt, general manager of the *Journal & Sentinel*, at a Thanksgiving party my senior year and said, "Bill, I wish you'd give Paxton a job." He'd agreed on the spot; people did not like to argue with my mother. After an interview next day Mr. Hoyt took me upstairs to meet Mr. Dure, the executive editor, who, after a long lecture on the fascinating adventures to which I could look forward as a reporter, led me across the newsroom to meet Mr. Bacon, the managing editor, who told me he knew my father, remembered me from my days as a stringer and would have a spot waiting for me on the *Journal* come June. No one asked me why I wanted to be a newspaperman, what my qualifications were or to fill out an application; no one told me to check in with personnel, there being no such department anyway; and I wrote it off to the proverbial eccentricity of the press that everyone in the newsroom wore a long, bushy beard, discovering only later that they were celebrating the city's centennial. By such casual happenstance was employment often accomplished in a simpler age.

Now here I was, six months later. The swinging double doors at the head of the stairs admitted me to a familiar scene. The newsroom occupied most of the second floor, a private office or two aside, and was in turn divided informally into separate areas for the *Journal*, the morning paper, and the *Twin City Sentinel*, which was published six afternoons a week; only the copy desk—a conglomeration of desks clustered to form a horseshoe around the large center post bearing the pneumatic ducts by which copy and proof passed between newsroom and composing room upstairs—was used by both. I spotted Mr. Bacon, who'd hired me, and he passed me on to Mr. Clingman, the city editor, who led me at once to an unoccupied desk, said, "Sit right down," and handed me a ten-inch stack of P.R. handouts with the instruction, "Here, do these." My initiation into the mysteries of modern journalism had begun.

Everything about a first job is new, but I was not altogether a newcomer. As a schoolboy I'd typed up my sports stories in one of the many newsroom cubicles of that time, now gone. Mr. Hoyt, the shrewd, cheerful little general manager who was actually the surrogate publisher in the absence of Gordon Gray, the owner, was an old friend of my parents'. Mr. Bacon, the managing editor, was Worth Bacon, a big, blond, shambling man prone to sudden bursts of anxiety about "missing the mails"—i.e., being too late for the midnight train that delivered the first run of the *Journal* to the mountain towns west of Winston-Salem; he had been around all my life, a respected local figure who knew almost everyone. Mr. Clingman, the city editor under whom I'd work directly, was Frank Clingman, a lifelong neighbor: six or seven years older than I, he'd grown up three doors down Oaklawn Avenue, a strapping lookalike to movie star Dennis Morgan so handsome my younger sister and her friends would sit on the curb in front of his house waiting for him to emerge; he was a journalism graduate of the University of North Carolina, a Coast Guard veteran and someone I seemed to have known—if at the distance inevitable between a little and a big boy—forever.

What I was supposed to do with the mimeographed handouts he'd dumped on my desk was less clear. Thumbing through them I found each marked "1 graf" or "2 graf" or occasionally even "3 graf," whatever a "graf" might be. Presently Pat Kelly came over to shake hands and welcome me aboard, a boy in my sister's school class I'd known for years, and he explained: a "graf" was a paragraph, and the scribbled instruction simply denoted the number of paragraphs to which each handout must be reduced. I rolled a long sheet of copy paper into the typewriter.

A moment later I rolled it out. Clingman brought over an equally long sheet of carbon paper, made the appropriate motions with his pipe and I started again. In Miss Mary Wiley's senior English at Reynolds High School I'd become an ace at writing précis—brief abstracts of longer prose pieces—and I prayed to recover the knack. The knack duly returned. I had enough experience to know a news lead from an epic poem, knew I must state who, what, when, where, and sometimes why or how, straightaway; but my "grafs" looked awkwardly long and I had no idea how the *Journal* handled such trivial but indispensable facts as titles, times, dates or street addresses—my versions seemed inconsistent. When I came to the end of the long sheet of copy paper I'd done half a dozen one- or two-paragraph stories, obviously no immediate threat to Dickens or Tolstoy. I'd also put the carbon paper in backward and imprinted the copy, neatly reversed, on the rear of the original. Clingman sighed tolerantly and said, "Well."

Things eased slightly as the afternoon progressed, but only slightly. I found it nearly impossible to remember which titles were capitalized, whether *cooperation*, *reoccurrence* and *weekend* were hyphenated and whether *street*, as in Spruce Street, should be abbreviated or spelled out. Clingman came over in midafternoon and handed me the *Journal & Sentinel* stylebook, as thick as a telephone directory, and told me the way to use it was to go through and memorize only what I wasn't doing already; but since I wasn't doing anything already but treading water I found that little help. At that point I was saved when I heard someone shout to Martin Howard, who was working at the copy desk a few feet away, "Does *congressman* go up or down in front of the son-of-a-bitch's name?" "Up" proved to mean you capitalized the first letter, "down" that you left it lowercase, and I took the point: when in doubt—more or less every third word—I should ask Martin Howard, a shy, bespectacled "rim man," or copyeditor, who was the resident authority on capitalization, abbreviation, punctuation, hyphenation, subject-verb agreement, English grammar in general and the innumerable peculiarities, contradictions, inconsistencies and logical absurdities of the *Journal & Sentinel* stylebook, a patient and agreeable man in his middle years who was the first of the many linguistic geniuses I was to meet on newspaper copy desks in coming years.

All the labels were new; the *Journal*, like every newspaper, used not only the conventional terminology of American journalism but its own lingo, and treasured it. When Clingman called to me to "check out the Southern planters" I drew a blank until someone at a nearby desk told me it meant I should ring the city's undertakers for "obits," i.e., obituaries. When Clingman instructed me during the evening to "get the ear" I had to ask to learn that I was to call the weather bureau at Smith Reynolds Airport for the data needed to fill next morning's front-page "weather ear," beside the "mast." But when I heard someone at the desk report loudly and with evident satisfaction that he'd "geesed the doodlum" I sensibly forbore to ask. All knowledge and wisdom, even what the "doodlum" was and what you did when you "geesed" it, would be revealed in the fullness of time.

By the end of the afternoon I'd begun to feel as much at home as if I'd worked at the *Journal* for years. The familiarity of the place and the presence of familiar faces helped; and though writing cut-down versions of business and civic-club handouts fell somewhat short of high adventure it forced me to learn at least the more common rules of *Journal* style, renewed what skill I had at condensation and—by focusing my attention on essentials—made me aware, as I needed to be, that I must separate, if need be ruthlessly, objective facts from promotion, special pleading or personal opinion. It was a lesson of profound importance, both intellectually and professionally, and there was nothing like reducing two pages of puff to two grafs of news to teach it. The *Journal*—in the person that afternoon of Frank Clingman—knew what it was doing.

The newsroom was as bustling with activity on Saturday as it was every other day, with the added pressure that the Sunday-morning paper was much larger than the rest; people came and went in a steady stream, and the noise—voices, typewriters, ringing telephones, the sounds of traffic on Marshall Street, heard through French windows thrown open as well to the heat and soot of downtown Winston-Salem—only abated during the dinner hour, but I soon grew accustomed to it. Keeping track of the people I met, hangers-on as well as colleagues, was harder. I knew Worth Bacon and Frank Clingman already, if only slightly, and Pat Kelly; but a large middle-aged man limping back and forth through the newsroom all afternoon was either a sportswriter or a tout, I couldn't remember which. The fellow at the desk to my left proved to be Rixie Hunter, whose byline I knew; and a friendly little fellow rolled over in his swivel chair—which I realized was the preferred mode of newsroom transit—introduced himself as Mark Ethridge and told me he was on his first day too, since he'd just surrendered reporting and the desk I now occupied for a stint on the copy desk, which he said he needed to learn. The big, broad, open-faced man at the desk behind me turned out to be Bill Woestendiek, another familiar byline, and presently the last staffer to report, Roy Thompson, whom I remembered from high school, came in from his initial run to the police station at city hall. All were about my age, give or take a year or so, and seemed immensely, _ _ _ ′al, though I got few of the jokes and wisecracks that passed ceaselessly; like the stylebook and "doodlum" they'd become clear, I supposed, when the dust settled.

It did not settle that evening, which grew busier and louder as the ten o'clock deadline for the first edition neared. Phones rang incessantly; pneumatic tubes whooshed off or thunked back from the composing room; Worth Bacon began to pace the floor, wringing his hands as he loudly lamented, "We'll miss the mails," though no one seemed to respond except to smile and go on working. Burrowing out at last from my handouts, I found myself taking fresh obits from area as well as local undertakers, disembodied voices from Lexington and Thomasville, Danbury and Walnut Cove, King, Pinnacle, Pilot Mountain, North Wilkesboro, Yadkinville, Elkin, Boone, Blowing Rock, West Jefferson and Sparta, towns south and west of Winston-Salem till then only names, dots on the map, now suddenly real because of a voice and a tone and sometimes a hound dog baying in the background. Obits were still, in that gentler time, not classified notices to be sold like used-car ads but legitimate news to be handled with respect; each got at least a brief story, at least a small headline, even the most obscure, and as the prominence rose the obit lengthened. I read back key details, spelled out survivors' names, often many, double-checked times and places of funerals and burials. At the *Journal* reporters were expected to get such things right.

The Sunday *Journal & Sentinel* bore the names of both papers but was produced by the *Journal* alone, and its many pages and several sections required advance planning and a staff larger than it looked, as well as—what I saw that first night on the job—plenty of last-minute hustle. But abruptly the newsroom went quiet, people got up from their desks and moved around, the "Sloppy Shoppe" vendor came through with his zinc wash pail of soft drinks and everybody relaxed; we'd made the mails again after all. The building rumbled, a boy came in to pass out fresh newspapers, warm and damp from the press, and we settled in to read for typos. Then, just as suddenly, it was eleven and time to quit.

For reasons I never learned, that summer Pat Kelly was managing a jazz combo playing at Staley's, a roadhouse out Stratford Road, and some of the others urged me to join them and their wives there for a beer and a bit of music. I called Nancy, whom I hadn't seen in months, picked her up at the ungodly hour of nearly midnight and off we went. Mark and Peg Ethridge had just had a baby, their first; Bill and Jo Woestendiek expected their first at any moment; there was much celebration. Pat Kelly's band was about what you'd expect of a newspaperman.

I went home half-drunk, but not on beer. I was as happy as I'd ever been in my life, exhilarated by my first day's work, overwhelmed by the warmth of my new friends and colleagues. My parents had gone to bed long since. The house was dark. I climbed the stairs to my room as quietly as I could, but not before folding a copy of the *Journal & Sentinel* across the banister just above the knob at the foot. Before leaving the newsroom I'd taken crayon in hand and proudly circled every story I'd written—all thirty-four, and not one of them longer than three inches.

18

I learned quickly that the rivalry between the *Journal* and *Sentinel*, and particularly between their staffs, was intense, heartfelt and regularly reinforced by their editors. It was a way of stimulating reporters to be even more ambitious and aggressive than most already were—of "motivating" them, in the jargon of a later time—and it worked. *Sentinel* reporters, most older, worked in the daytime and had their weekends free, which we on the *Journal*, tough, brilliant and adventurous in our own eyes, regarded as sissy; and the brevity of their time on the street, nine till noon at best, prevented them from developing the fully rounded stories we believed characteristic of the more comprehensive *Journal*. *Sentinel* staffers, for their part, seemed to think the *Journal* was peopled with zany young gumshoes and show-offs trying

to win prizes and invitations to join the *New York Times*;
besides, it was obvious, we had more fun.

There was some truth to both views, especially to the
suspicion that we had more fun; but not much. Mostly
the competition was synthetic, a kind of ritualistic rhe-
torical calisthenics unconsciously but inevitably designed to compensate for the fact that neither paper had
any real competition. In the absence of other morning or
afternoon dailies within the area immediately north,
south and west of Winston-Salem, with radio news a by-
product of our copy and local television still a glimmer in
the distance, the *Journal & Sentinel*—or, to state it more
exactly, the Piedmont Publishing Company—had read-
ers and advertisers under uncontested control.

American newspaper publishers, almost all of whom
enjoy similar blessings, do not like to be reminded that
they rule monopolies, a word at which they wince, pre-
ferring instead to call their properties "consolidations"
and to speak with pride of the improvement mergers
have brought to the collection of news, the development
of printing and dissemination technology and the elevation of journalistic ethics and responsibility. Much of
this pride is justified, for the elimination of the self-
destructive waste inevitable to difficult competition has
brought many of the benefits they claim; but it does not
change the fact that a local newspaper monopoly—often

a near-monopoly over electronic media as well—leaves them the only vehicle of information and advertising in town.

The monopolization of the American press is by now too complete to lament or applaud; and the Winston-Salem newspapers were a classic case. Both of the small towns whose growth and eventual merger made them a single bustling industrial city had boasted small competitive newspapers of an astonishingly varied quality in the nineteenth and early twentieth centuries. The rising costs of publication and news gathering had forced increasingly bitter rivalries among them for advertising revenues in a limited market, however, and one by one they had bought each other out, the penultimate result being two papers, one morning, the other afternoon, which finally merged beneath the aegis of the Piedmont Publishing Company. The company itself was mostly owned by Gordon Gray, one of the sons of Bowman Gray, president of Reynolds Tobacco, though by my time service in World War II, then in Washington public life, had removed him from daily supervision of the company and left it in the hands of his surrogate, W. K. Hoyt, general manager. But Gordon Gray's influence remained palpable. He was a benevolent rich man who had bought the papers primarily to end what he believed to be ruinous partisanship; he regarded the press as essentially a public utility with strong responsibilities to the welfare of the community; and he saw to it, even from afar, that the *Journal* and *Sentinel* were fair, disinterested and balanced in their coverage and editorial policies. (Sometimes this produced humorous results, as when the *Journal*, its editorial-page editor a rock-ribbed Baptist "dry," editorially opposed bringing state liquor stores to Winston-Salem, while his opposite number on the *Sentinel*, younger and less puritanical, used his page to promote them.) Under Gray's ownership the papers had become respected local institutions, and their editors and reporters, if not precisely loved, had won the grudging toleration of local business and political leaders, though of course the toleration waxed and waned with the oxes we gored.

I confess I thought rarely about such matters in the summer of 1949. Like most novices then or later I knew almost nothing about the profession I'd entered so blithely: nothing, specifically, about the history and role of the press; nothing about the *Journal & Sentinel* beyond its familiarity and its hospitality to me; nothing about the Establishment of Winston-Salem or how the newspapers fit into it, or didn't; nothing, indeed, about the practice of journalism beyond the fact that Hemingway, Mencken, Stephen Crane, Kipling and numerous other writers I idolized had got their start as reporters, loved being newspapermen and, even when famous, returned to war or political correspondence from time to time. For me, at twenty-four, it was romantic adventure, and that was enough.

I settled quickly into the schedule. Though dramatic news is almost always unforeseeable the greater number of events worth reporting arise from the routine operations of government and business and are thus discovered by routine. As a fledgling reporter—I never heard the expression "cub reporter" used on a newspaper—I was assigned a "beat," a round of offices, institutions and occasionally persons I must check regularly, more or less daily. Mine comprised, among many smaller fish, the chamber of commerce, the retail merchants association, major banks, a few key individuals here and there— barbers, bootblacks, shopkeepers, hotel, bank and office clerks, a few well-placed and often well-known executives—who were especially knowledgable and curious and who, experience had shown, were good sources of information on events all over the city that were unlikely to surface by ordinary means; their names rarely appeared in the papers, but their tips were generally accurate and often of immense value. They were the true "insiders."

Along with most of the other *Journal* reporters I came to work at two, as the last run of the *Sentinel* shook the sidewalks in every direction, checked with Clingman for particular assignments or to clear with him what I anticipated finding that afternoon, then set out to cover the beat. Beforehand most of us drank coffee down the street, and many of the most helpful things I learned that summer I picked up then, from Bill Woestendiek and Hoke Norris and Rixie Hunter; but I was on my own after that and had to teach myself—or beg the mercy of others—the ordinary elements of the work I'd elected to do.

They did not teach such things at Johns Hopkins, or even at the journalism schools from which several of my colleagues had graduated, and there was no reason they should or way they could. The principles of orderly composition are universal and can be learned by drill; but most of what precedes the writing depends on curiosity, persistence, a knack for both listening and hearing and a second sense for nuance, hint and implication, all of them personal traits generally inborn and usually sharpened by experience but beyond the abstractions and generalizations of the classroom. I had an aptitude for abstraction and generalization and was forever grateful to my Hopkins mentors for bringing it out, but it was useless when I was trying to get Harry Krusz, the vigorous, charming and wily executive director of the chamber of commerce, to spill the beans on some new business settling in Winston-Salem.

To such tasks I brought imperfect skills. I was already at least competent as a writer and had little difficulty learning the particular principles of newspaper prose; I was voraciously curious about what people and institutions did and how they worked and I listened well enough for a beginner. But I was not as persistent as I needed to be—it embarrassed me to embarrass others with questions they obviously did not want to answer; and I frequently failed, however intently I listened, to hear what was between, behind and beneath the words I got as answers. I was hardly shy, and I took immense and immediate relish in discovering how my native city was run; but it would take weeks and months of experience—as well as a measure of the hardening produced by the realization that my curiosity, the *Journal*'s curiosity, was justified by the sound political principle that public business is the public's business—before I became comfortable in pressing for information. I had yet to understand that most officials, in government and business alike, define news as good or bad exclusively by how flattering it is to themselves.

In making my rounds I was greatly helped from the start by being not only a local boy but the son of prominent parents. I knew the streets by heart, the buildings, the offices and many of the sources I called on, some of them as well as a young man can know a mature adult; and it often happened that even when I didn't they knew me or my name because they knew or knew of my father and mother. It is impossible for me to exaggerate or forget, all these many years later, how much it eased my way. I was absurdly innocent of worldliness, had no idea how important being known could be and never dreamed of using my parents' names to open doors. But I did not have to; they opened anyway; and I was spared much of the initial awkwardness every young reporter feels on his first beat because my parents' position inevitably preceded and supported me. It was a piece of luck I had not foreseen and did not fully appreciate at the time, but it got me off to a promising start.

My rounds ended, like most reporters', at five, when offices closed. The next hour or so, in the newsroom, was one of the busiest of the day. Most of the routine news we'd gathered during the afternoon had to be written then; if some stories required follow-up or confirming calls it was necessary, if at all possible, to make them then, before sources scattered for the evening; tabulations—lists, statistical summaries, the police-court docket—had to be double-checked by reading copy to another reporter. It was important to get early copy written, edited and sent "upstairs," to the composing room, before six, to leave time for covering evening meetings or pursuing longer stories after the dinner hour. It was not uncommon to write a dozen stories or more between five and six.

By then the newsroom staff was complete, the police reporter and copy-desk men having come in during the later part of the afternoon; and we dined—almost everyone at home—in shifts. After dinner things got frantic again. Phones rang constantly. Some reporters went out to cover night meetings. Roy Thompson, the police reporter, chased fire trucks, ambulances and squad cars as signals announced emergencies. We took obits, stories called in by stringers throughout the *Journal*'s circulation area, crank calls tipping us off to flying saucers, Hitler sightings in Southside, incipient scandals everywhere; we finished up stories still hanging from the afternoon. At odd moments, if any, we dug for or worked on "anytime" copy, for it was a *Journal* requirement, reinforced daily by Frank Clingman's invariable "What you got for Sunday?" that every reporter turn in at least two features to fill the largest edition of the week.

Abruptly at ten, as I'd discovered my first night, things quietened. The first-edition deadline had come and gone. Reporters slowed, drank Cokes, wandered around chatting. Deskmen, called by loud bangs on the pneumatic tubes, went "upstairs" to oversee makeup. Now and then a ringing phone brought a late obit. At eleven most of us folded and wandered off—for a beer, a late date, occasionally even home.

Most days alternated boredom and exhilaration in an odd mélange of routine and frenzy. Few of us ended them as tired as we should have been or as sleepy as most people feel nearing midnight. The routine was a safety net as well as an illusion—necessary both to guarantee coverage of the known and to slow the flow of adrenaline when the unexpected happened. No two days were ever quite alike. News varied in quantity and interest with the seasons and—we came to believe—the moon. The parade of people with whom we talked changed constantly. Wholly surprising events, some the stuff of pulp fiction, occurred almost nightly. I'd been at work a week when an anonymous caller, reaching my phone by chance, tipped me to "something queer" at a flophouse a block away. There I found the sort of meaningless story every reporter loves: a tenant, dreaming he'd been robbed, woke up to discover he really had. The police were puzzled but bored. Not I. I got the facts, raced back to the newsroom and wrote fast enough to make the second edition—and bagged what was in those days the ultimate reward: my first byline.

19

Bylines were far from common in American newspapers, and in the *Journal*, in 1949, and even when given for a particular story were not to be taken for granted. Generally they were reserved for unusual enterprise or originality and were bestowed ad hoc by the city and copy desks to give special recognition—or call special attention—to pieces the editors deemed of superior merit. An experienced reporter could go weeks without one, then have several in a row, or have a dozen stories or more in a single edition but a byline on only one—or none. The *Journal* believed rarity preserved value.

I make the point not only to explain my own elation at my first byline but to illustrate the *Journal*'s austerity in matters of presentation. Newspaper reporters, while appreciated, were professionals of whom dependable performance might be assumed, not the stars they would later become, and the *Journal* held them to strict standards. Personality journalism—which became epidemic after Watergate, and in response to the show-biz aura of television news—was not encouraged. The ideal of journalistic objectivity, though everyone acknowledged its practical impossibility, was nonetheless preached and sought: editors and deskmen made every effort to eradicate personal bias, whether of opinion, sentiment or even assumption, from news copy; identification of a particular reporter with a particular subject, even if it conferred the cachet of expertise, was avoided lest it imply special status; the aim was, if possible, to produce a daily newspaper boasting its own institutional quality and integrity, not merely an anthology of star turns. The effort was doomed, of course: human fallibility, personal frailty, individual ambition and the urge to shine make objectivity and impersonality easier to state than attain. The *Journal*, in practice, had already acknowledged this, if only implicitly, by permitting one staffer, Roy Thompson, to win such audience popularity with his offbeat features and one-sentence, one-paragraph style that his local stardom was established. But for the rest it sought to make the paper seamless, an art that concealed art, a newspaper in which any story could have been written, if necessary, by anyone on the staff.

This fastidious concern for detail was expressed with particular force in the paper's attention to writing and editing. The *Journal*'s stylebook proved the least of it: I quickly absorbed the major points of capitalization, abbreviation and punctuation and could count on the copy desk to spot the less obvious oversights. What proved more demanding was the elimination of words and phrases connoting unspoken bias—I had to learn to take special care, in reporting what sources said or claimed, not to seem to endorse it. This was best served by quoting directly as often as possible, but sometimes paraphrase or summary was inevitable, and I took great pains to make it clear I neither agreed nor disagreed. Jim Rush, the hawk-eyed, hawk-beaked telegraph editor and chief of the copy desk, was a zealous taskmaster about such distinctions, as he was about language generally. He was an alumnus of Williams, had done graduate work at Columbia and taught English at Colby before coming to Winston-Salem, and he was both an accomplished and an unsparing grammarian who let nothing unseemly pass his editing pencil; more than once I watched with fear and trembling as he left the slot of the copy desk to show me this error or that in my copy, always explaining patiently but emphatically why what I had written, however small the matter seemed to me, left a suggestion of acquiescence or disapproval. He insisted that people "believed" rather than "thought" things, and that they died "unexpectedly," not "suddenly." ("Everybody dies suddenly," he said. "One minute they're alive and the next they're dead.") One night he gave me a lesson in relative pronouns and restrictive versus nonrestrictive clauses ("When you use 'which' when you should use 'that' you sound like 'Duffy's Tavern'") that reddened my face but cured me of an embarrassing blunder. Like every editor from Worth Bacon down to the newest deskman he strove to create a newspaper as respectable in usage as the prissiest high-school English teacher and as impartial as a telephone book. None of them ever quite succeeded in publishing the perfect paper, but perfection was the goal; and the result, night after night, was clean, clear exposition as free of clichés, jargon and the triteness of most newspapers as human hands could hope to make, a paper that—as Tom Wicker, soon to join the *Journal*, wrote years later in his book *On Press*—reflected the *Journal*'s "high standards on apparently small matters." It followed, Wicker added, that "high standards on details almost dictate high standards on larger matters" and that high standards "strongly sustained are the best guarantee of high morale and pride in the ranks."

Both morale and pride were indeed high, and the result was a daily newspaper of medium size (a circulation of slightly more than sixty-five thousand) that was the envy of every newspaperman in North Carolina. It regularly won prizes for reporting and typography and was frequently praised in the national trade press for its initiative and independence. The immediate credit went to its staff, of course, but less visible was the role of men whose names rarely appeared in print. Preeminent among them was Gordon Gray, the owner, who though physically present only rarely insisted on protecting the newspaper's quality and autonomy and to do so ploughed its profits back into the product. The confidence this inspired in his employees was palpable, and his spokesman on the scene, general manager Bill Hoyt, good-humoredly and wisely reinforced his principles. Managing editor Worth Bacon, though something of a fussbudget, was as skillful a copyeditor as North Carolina journalism had, as well as a seasoned observer of events whose judgments on the relative importance of stories ensured fair emphasis, proportion and balance in the play the *Journal* gave them. Leon Dure, the executive editor who'd given me my job, was gone by the time I arrived, the beneficiary of a family inheritance, but his flamboyant enthusiasm for the newspaper had created its young, ambitious and almost hyperkinetic staff; and Wallace Carroll, who succeeded him and came on board the same week as I, oversaw every aspect of the daily schedule with an eye practiced by years of experience all over the world.

Wally Carroll—though I would not have dreamed of calling him anything but "Mr. Carroll"—was an interesting contrast to Dure. Where Dure was a schemer and dreamer whose daily monologues inspired his underlings, with the fervor of Henry V on St. Crispin's Day, to romantic exploits, Carroll, sober, bespectacled, was the master of reportorial detail with a strong sense of the overall product. His presence was calm, measured, precise. As a European correspondent for the United Press before World War II he'd covered high-level politics and diplomacy, and his wartime service with the Office of War Information had deepened his understanding of what was coming to be called "geopolitics." His book about the OWI, *Persuade or Perish*, was authoritative, and his experience and good sense gave the *Journal* both perspective and depth, to all of which he added a crisp, lucid writing style that permitted him to make the unfamiliar complexities of world events clear and to step in, when necessary, and untangle the syntactical knots in local copy. Both he and Dure were gifted editors, however different in look and manner, whose leadership raised the aspirations of their followers. I shudder to remember how much sleep my youthful hijinks must have cost Carroll. It was his custom to leave blue slips on the bulletin board noting goofs, gaffes and oversights in that morning's *Journal*, a considerable share of which, alas, were for me.

Neither of us had been at the paper more than a month when I stumbled across a story—or had it stumble across me—that would keep the *Journal* in hot water for the rest of the summer. Early one morning my mother woke me for a telephone call. In a quivering voice that was both frightened and angry an elderly man told me there was "real trouble" at the County Hospital and I ought to "look into it." I knew nothing about the County Hospital and less about how Forsyth County was governed, but a few calls to nurses whose names my informant had given me suggested "real trouble" was indeed in progress. I checked with city editor Frank Clingman, who had to be roused too, and he told me to get going.

The trouble was that a number of nurses at the hospital had complained to the chief of staff of dubious medical practices and drunken misconduct by a staff physician and surgeon whose credentials were mysterious anyway. The County Hospital was a threadbare collection of ramshackle buildings in the country, a last refuge for the indigent sick, the sort of institution that has now all but vanished. The disgruntled nurses, eager to talk for the record after being rebuffed by the chief physician and then by the board of county commissioners, told similar stories—of surgery conducted by the doctor while drunk, abuse of patients, sloppy prescription of drugs—their superiors had discounted out of hand. They sounded convincing, but we had not even gone into print with the story when the commissioners elevated what might have been a minor mess into a serious local scandal: they fired the nurses.

I was in over my head from the outset. No reportorial experience had prepared me to handle so complex a story involving so many contending allegations and denials. I was quick enough to smell it out, energetic enough to pursue it and self-confident enough to believe I could make it stick; but I was still far too green to know how to reach all the points of view I needed to keep it fair or to have mastered the literary skill to produce an unfolding account in a balanced, coherent manner. Wally Carroll and Worth Bacon rescued me by putting Bill Woestendiek on the story with me—most editors would have given it to him outright and sent me back to covering the orphans' picnic in Mocksville—and together, as the days passed, we dug up more scandal than we'd originally realized was there. Before the story ended in September with the overdue dismissal of the alcoholic doctor the commissioners sought to pressure the *Journal* into what Wally Carroll, in a signed front-page piece, called a "conspiracy of silence"; I was thrown off the County Hospital grounds by an irate deputy; a Forsyth County grand jury was instructed to investigate the case; and Bill Woestendiek and I, acting mostly on hunch, unearthed the fact—by calling county seats all over eastern North Carolina—that the "doctor" was a fraud convicted of practicing medicine without a license the year before. He was the product of an unaccredited medical school whose credentials for serving on the medical staff of a public hospital, or any other, no one in authority had bothered to check. At that revelation the commissioners, by then thoroughly tainted with stupidity, carelessness and arrogance, folded.

I loved it, every overwrought and possibly overblown minute. Alongside such later scandals as Watergate and Iran-Contra it was small potatoes: no one had died, no one had run off with the county treasury, no bribes had passed; the principal revelation, that Forsyth County was governed by idiots, was hardly surprising. But I relished the story and missed it when it had ended. It was a genuine *local* scandal, and local news was the specialty of the *Journal*; besides, it was exciting. Every young reporter loves to play sleuth, and most older ones too if their legs have held out: loves to chase fire trucks, answer police calls, hang out with detectives; it is his business as surely as it is a dog's to bury bones and tree cats, fusing the thrill of pursuit, the exposure of dark deeds and the extraordinary satisfaction of overweening self-righteousness. It was an adventure in which I could indulge my Raymond Chandler–Humphrey Bogart fantasies day and night, and I was still boy enough to live half the time in an imagined world of heroes and villains, primary colors and moral absolutes. The consideration that throughout the whole month of derring-do I'd given not a moment's sympathy to the poor drunken soul whose desperate bad judgment had caused all the trouble did not occur to me till years afterward.

I had other reasons to love the episode. It confirmed my choice of profession. It brought me headlong into the cockpit of public institutions and the men who ran them and brought me my first realization that most of them do it badly. It exercised my native wit and ingenuity. It gave me something bigger to write about than the chamber of commerce. Above all, I believe, it moved my own writing forward. In such free time as I had I was trying to start a novel. Memories of India and the army would not let me be, in particular the tale of a black American soldier from a nearby outfit who'd killed an officer, escaped into the Naga Hills and lived for a time among the headhunters, and eventually been captured and hanged at the Ledo stockade. I saw it clearly in my mind but had no idea how to organize or compose it, and opening page after opening page, laboriously typed and crossed out on yellow second sheets, sailed into the wastebasket of my boyhood room. My adventure at the County Hospital somehow helped. It did not, like a bolt of lightning, abruptly clarify my confused thoughts or project the right words to get me going. But it strengthened my confidence that I could handle a narrative longer than three paragraphs; it eased my way.

20

At a salary of forty-five dollars a week I was unable to take my holidays on the Riviera; but I was having so much fun the possibility did not occur to me anyway, and my paychecks accumulated in my wallet until one day the business office called and asked me please to cash them. I did, whereupon my savings account began to grow: I simply hadn't time to spend money, and living at home, with my parents, kept my expenses modest. In retrospect it embarrasses me to realize how thoughtlessly I took their hospitality for granted, but it was common to do so till one was paid enough to stand on one's feet, even for newlyweds.

Low wages were a perennial feature of newspaper work; but like almost every single person on the *Journal* I probably would have paid to be there. Hoke Norris, a dozen years older than I and at thirty-eight the senior *Journal* reporter in skill as well as age, told me he'd started at ten dollars a week with the Associated Press upon graduating from Wake Forest in the depths of the Depression and was happy to have it, and I suspect most of the older hands could have told similar tales. The basic truth was that newspapering was less a means to earn a living than a way of life in itself, a silent brotherhood sharing a secret understanding. Over the decades that followed, in fact, few of us ever seriously tried anything else. As the old saying went, it beat working.

A newspaper job—at least on the news and editorial side—meant belonging to a society of extraordinarily independent men and women who neither could nor would join the mainstream of American middle-class life. We were often called "bohemian," and no doubt we were, though it was a bohemianism not of beads, beards, odd dress and a jargon of dissent but of an instinctive skepticism, an indifference to accepted institutions and a critical intelligence that viewed most of society's behavior as either comic or criminal and sometimes both. Few of the newspapermen I knew, on the *Journal* or elsewhere, deliberately invited attention or sought to provoke argument, and most lived their domestic lives conventionally enough; but few cared much for the greasy ambitions or the getting and spending they saw around them. Happily or miserably, well or poorly, they lived in their minds and in the piles of books they accumulated like paper clips and rubber bands, and they retained a quizzical, distinctly unimpressed opinion of bourgeois values and aspirations—romantic cynics, observers, outsiders to the end.

Within their circle, however, the outsiders became insiders, privy to an extraordinary range of shared backgrounds, beliefs, assumptions, interests and prejudices. I had never been taken up or accepted so quickly, feeling after a week or two I'd known these friends forever. We had, it seemed, almost everything in common: we'd all been to good colleges and edited publications there; most of us had been in the war, and the ones who hadn't were either too disabled or too young; we came from educated families in which argument about politics and religion was encouraged, rather than banned, and books were valued and read; we liked politicians but distrusted them (all officeholders were assumed to be corrupt till proven honest); and we all intended to challenge Hemingway (or Faulkner or Hardy or Wolfe) with novels of our own, the uncorrected and unfinished drafts of which gathered silverfish and dust in the bottom drawers of our desks. We liked to debate, to solve the political problems of the postwar world, to swap tall tales. We believed we were the brightest people in Winston-Salem and deserved higher pay than the *Journal* was likely to offer us. We liked to stay up late drinking beer and moonshine and listening to *South Pacific* and *Kiss Me Kate*. We liked to party.

The partying was innocent but regular. Hardly a Saturday arrived but Pat Kelly tacked a note to the bulletin board inviting everyone, and anyone anyone wanted to bring, to Hoke's or Bill's or Maggie's or Hal's, starting at eleven (out of deference to the poor sods on the Saturday trick) and continuing indefinitely. Plenty of beer was on ice, occasionally something stronger (Forsyth County was still dry, so buying liquor necessitated a run to the next county), and someone usually remembered to bring pretzels or potato chips. We played records, smoked and argued, now and then breaking the pontification—when he wasn't there—with imitations of Worth Bacon fretting about the mails. Sooner or later Pat Kelly passed the hat to reimburse the host, a dollar a head being the established hit, and the party normally ended at or near dawn when Frank Spencer, the night-blooming sports editor, arrived with half a dozen cops just off duty, their siren wailing, and they all made a groaning breakfast table of scrambled eggs and hot cakes for the hearty few still awake. Neighbors rarely complained. I'd never heard better talk or had a better time.

Besides being warm and hospitable my new friends

seemed—and proved, both at the *Journal* and in their subsequent careers—to be highly gifted newspapermen and -women. Pat Kelly, from Winston-Salem, was an effervescent and vigorous colleague; a graduate of the University of North Carolina, he'd edited the *Daily Tar Heel*, that campus's most envied job, and he aimed at a career as an editor, which eventually, in Raleigh and Atlanta and finally on his own small-town paper, he became. Mark Ethridge, whose reportorial spot I'd taken, was preparing for editorial work, and ended as editorial-page editor of the *Detroit Free Press*; son of a famous newspaperman, whose visits to Winston-Salem always occasioned a party, he'd grown up in the liberal journalism of the *Louisville Courier-Journal*, and his education had been honed at Princeton. Jim Rush, who ran the copy desk with a ferocious demand for daily perfection, was a voluntary emigrant to North Carolina from his native New England; no one on the paper had a better eye for the subtleties of English grammar or a better command of the tools available to display news effectively. Hal Levy was another newspaper son, a graduate of Washington and Lee whose editing talents, first as telegraph and then as Sunday editor, deepened the cultural quality of the *Journal*'s feature coverage; he was a workaholic who put in longer hours than anyone else, all to the advantage of the paper. I learned from them all, as

I did from Rixie Hunter, Jim McEwen and Roy Thompson, all of whom were already on board when I arrived.

The *Journal & Sentinel*, like most American newspapers, had always employed women as reporters and editors, and the wartime shortage of men had greatly increased their numbers; but unlike many another paper it kept most of the women on afterward. The result was the development of a substantial crew of outstanding women in news areas beyond the traditional society or women's pages. The *Sentinel* shone with Mary Garber, one of the nation's first women to cover sports, and with Frances Griffin. None shone more brightly than Bonnie Angelo, with whom I'd grown up; tiny, irrepressibly cheerful and vigorous, she was women's editor when I got there but moved to the news side and from it to a distinguished career with Long Island's *Newsday*, then *Time*, for which she covered everything from the White House to Whitehall. Marjorie Hunter, universally known as "Maggie," was another who started on the women's side, but she quickly came over to straight news and progressed from the *Journal* to the Washington bureau of the *New York Times*; her parties were among the best, and the longest-lasting. Lucille Cathey, who arrived at the *Journal* a few months after me, was a solid and dependable reporter too, though I was mortified—perhaps more mortified than she—when, on her first day, I took her to the courthouse, where, as we entered the large courtroom, the prosecutor in what turned out to be a rape case asked, in a voice that could have been heard in China, "And did he wear a *condom*?" In that politer, more innocent and infinitely more circumspect time, as well as at the polite and circumspect if not altogether innocent *Journal*, the word *condom* was rarely heard, and never in public.

My two closest early *Journal* friends got there ahead of me.

Hoke Norris was a native North Carolinian, raw-boned and towheaded, who was the son of a Baptist minister and a graduate of Wake Forest, in those days known with both affection and asperity as "Baptist Hollow." But Baptist austerities and rigidities, which gave North Carolina its air of puritanism till well into the 1950s, seemed not to have touched him; he was defiantly agnostic and a two-fisted connoisseur of spirits in the best newspaper tradition—no mean feat in a state where the Baptist vote created a bewildering system of "local option," in which one could go from wet to dry simply by crossing a county line. Assigned to city hall, the *Journal*'s best beat, he was the de facto political reporter as well, and his prewar years in Raleigh with the Associated Press and the *Raleigh News & Observer* (known throughout the state as the "Nuisance and Disturber") had given him a degree of political sophistication and the sort of political contacts no one at the *Journal*, and few in the entire state, could rival. But he was also a cultivated, enlightened writer whose wide reading, wartime experience as an intelligence officer in the South Pacific and ear for the rhythms of English prose made his copy literate, cogent, authoritative and invariably interesting. He too wrote fiction, had published short stories in "little" magazines and was working on a novel, and in 1950 he became the first North Carolina newspaperman to win a Nieman Fellowship, which gave him a free year at Harvard but deprived the rest of us of his brilliant company; for he and his wife, Edna, a dead ringer for actress Mary Astor, were inveterate and indefatigable hosts and revelers in the ongoing *Journal* party.

Bill Woestendiek was only a year older than I but already a *Journal* veteran. He too was a Carolina journalism graduate and *Daily Tar Heel* editor, but he was no Tar Heel himself except by adoption, hailing in fact from upstate New York. He was as Dutch, in name, look and manner, as Hoke was English yeoman or I Scotch quarreler: a big bear of a man, tall, broad-chested, with a wide, agreeable, nearly naive face that attracted the confidences of news sources and friends alike. But he was far from naive, possessing a shrewdness and quick wit that had brought him within a year to the courthouse beat, where he covered not only superior court, an almost full-time assignment in itself, but county government—commissioners, schools, the sheriff's office, the labyrinthine duties of the county clerk, the county attorney and register of deeds, indeed anything that popped up in his bailiwick, including the local lawyer, known to everyone as "Chain Gang," who regularly stole soft drinks and small change from the blind woman who ran the snack stand in the courthouse lobby, an act that we all agreed perfectly symbolized his profession.

Two other close friends came to the *Journal* after me.

Walt Friedenberg, another Baptist minister's son and Wake Forest graduate, was tall, still as awkward as an adolescent and given to throwaway jokes that few people got but that revealed a bright, well-stocked mind still absorbing knowledge and impressions more rapidly than he yet knew how to use them. Like me but few others on the staff he was still single, and we hung out together after work, having midnight eggs and bacon at the Toddle House, drinking beer and listening to music in a little studio I'd put together in what had once been the servant's room in my parents' garage, above all crashing the occasional late-night convention parties on the roof of the Hotel Robert E. Lee, across the street and up half a block from the paper. We'd cadge drinks and dance with the girls many of the conventioneers—dentists, realtors, restauranteurs, lawyers—had brought with them, since by the time we arrived they were generally too drunk to care. We generally expressed our thanks with enthusiastic if less than professional renditions of the songs—sometimes *all* the songs—from *Kiss Me Kate*. Once, invited to protract the party in a private room, we entered only to find a fairly soused Worth Bacon, our boss, with a blonde on one arm and a redhead on the other. We left quickly and hoped he'd forget.

Tom Wicker, who came up from the sandhills of North Carolina, was still another Carolina alumnus. Big-boned, strong and as blond as Hoke, but with the pug-nosed, open face of a small boy, he worked first on the rim of the copy desk, where every night, as if by ritual, he marked the passing of the last first-edition copy upstairs by drawing a spiral notebook from the drawer and proceeding, oblivious to all else, to write in it with a copy pencil. When, headed out to look for beer and girls, we asked, "Great American Novel?" he invariably grinned and nodded and went on writing. A year or so later Gold Medal Books, the first line of paperback originals, published the lurid thriller *Get Out of Town* by one "Paul Connolly," who soon proved to be none other than our colleague and friend from the copy desk. Three or four equally lurid Paul Connolly works soon followed, among them one printed by mistake in a huge overrun for which Gold Medal, which paid a cent a copy *printed*, had to cough up a much fatter check than usual. All of that and a Nieman year at Harvard behind him, Wicker wrote a big fiction about North Carolina politics, *The Kingpin*, under his own name, and had the remarkable experience of having reviewers praise it as a "brilliant first novel."

Though he looked like a country boy—and retains to this day the simple courtesy of his origins—Wicker was no hayseed. He worked hard, read all night (and later took to sitting up till dawn in round-the-clock movies) and could handle any task on the paper. Though none of us could foresee where his gifts would take him we knew he had the rare connective intelligence that sees events in contexts, as well as the liberal political sympathies common to our profession and a fluent literary ability that could focus and illuminate in a few hundred words; so it was no surprise when he became chief of the Washington bureau of the *New York Times*, a columnist for its Op-Ed page and the author of a whole series of novels and books of nonfiction, all of the greatest distinction but none by the mysterious and pseudonymous Paul Connolly.

21

We did not know it then, but we were at the end of an era in American newspapers. A technological revolution that would replace mechanical production with typesetting, printing and news transmission done by electronics and computers was already under way and would reach its culmination, changing everything, by the 1970s. But in the late 1940s and early 1950s "hot" type was still being set by Linotype and Ludlow, page forms were still being cast by stereotype and the composing room and pressroom were still the province of noise, dirt, heat and powerful labor unions representing highly skilled compositors and printers who served long apprenticeships to master their demanding, delicate tasks. They were blue-collar and we white-; they lived in working-class neighborhoods and we in the green, shaded suburbs of the professional class; they were educated by experience and we in colleges. But their physical toughness—and their vigorous pride in the product they got out in multiple editions thirteen times a week—gave a newspaper, gave the *Journal & Sentinel*, a heartiness of atmosphere in which all of us worked.

That atmosphere was rich in personality and eccentricity, a bit bohemian at times, and much of it was deeply comic, for newspapers had a strong attraction for rebellious men and women, some highly gifted as well, who had no affection for the more conventional callings of the workaday world. No one ever caught this better than Hecht and MacArthur in their famous play *The Front Page*, which, though heightened, conveyed perfectly the strange blend of romanticism, adventurousness and delight in outrageous pranks that characterized so much of a newspaperman's day. In 1949 reporters and editors, underpaid and often regarded as suspicious nonconformists, still displayed much of that delight in thumbing their noses at the metronomic banalities by which it seemed to them most Americans lived. Bob Casey, a famous Chicago reporter of the Hecht-MacArthur era, had an illustrative anecdote: when a polite old lady remarked that in his profession he must meet "such interesting people," he answered, "Yes, ma'am, and all of them are newspapermen."

The *Journal* was like that. Its casual hospitality to eccentricity encouraged extremes of personality that would have seemed dramatic license, and realistically improbable, in a Frank Capra movie. Frank Jones, the senior photographer, was a Winston-Salem native who knew everyone in town, high, low, white and black, and made it his trademark to insult the subjects of his expert camera with scathing, often scabrous observations about their appearance, taste, sex lives and probable ancestry, the result being a popularity, in the newsroom and outside it, no one on the staff could approach. Hobble McMichael, the clubfooted gambler I'd seen limping around the newsroom my first night there, agreeably answered phones, took messages and sometimes wrote brief, incomprehensible obits and sports shorts when no one else was around to do it, though, being neither on staff nor a quite respectable citizen, he was only a hanger-on and pal of the sports editor. Mike Mullen, an itinerant copyeditor who drifted drunkenly but cheerfully in and out of newsrooms all over the South, generally began his day by meticulously sharpening the thirty or forty copy pencils he carried with him, each bearing the masthead of a different paper he'd worked for; this struck some as a waste of company time, but those who knew better knew that he was a master grammarian and stylist who could clarify and sharpen almost any story and who was said, after being instructed in the mysteries and curiosities of the *Richmond Times-Dispatch* stylebook, to have stood up, pocketed his famous pencils and stalked from the building, pausing only at the head of the stairs to turn and proclaim contemptuously that he would "never work for a newspaper that declines to hyphenate *co-operate*."

Among the many strange fish who swam through the newsroom, or worked in it, were a check-suited carnival press agent who annually distributed passes to the girlie shows, with whispered advice on when "they'll take it all off," and annually admonished us to remember that his name was Snellens, "which is spelled the same way backward as forward"; a threadbare lawyer who badgered the city desk for tips on fire and ambulance calls; and an ancient, dusty crone who was our stringer in Pinnacle and Pilot Mountain, wanted to be paid in silver and inspired numerous imitations, all based on the Wicked Witch of the West, as she tottered, brandishing her umbrella and cursing the *Journal* for its parsimony, into the night.

This zoo of oddballs provided us an unending vaudeville of amusement and wonder, but its indisputable masters were two veteran *Journal* staffers long since elevated to the empyrean as Winston-Salem characters of unchallengeable color and flavor.

Nutt Caldwell, officially state editor but in fact the presiding figure in the newsroom, bore the baptismal name of Gowan, but it was impossible to think of him as anything so dignified, and in fact not even his wife or sisters, all of them perfectly normal and respectable, ever called him that. By the time I knew him he was a chunky man of middle age and middle height with wiry, graying black hair and glasses the thickness of greasy-spoon tumblers, but he could spot an idle reporter across town and seldom let anything in the newsroom escape his notice or robust public comment. "Lock the doors!" he'd bellow at the sight of Hobble McMichael limping through the swinging louvers at the top of the stairs. "Check your wallets!" Or he'd say, "All the bars must be closed," when Frank Spencer, the sports editor, with whom he'd alternated roles as comic and straight man for a quarter of a century, stumbled in with his customary entourage of bookies, street freaks and layabouts. Technically, I suppose, managing editor Worth Bacon and city editor Frank Clingman outranked him in the *Journal* pecking order, but no one ever doubted—least of all they—that it was Nutt Caldwell's newsroom. Nor would they have wanted it otherwise: his spirit, humor and warmth made it one of the pleasantest places on earth.

He renamed everything and everyone with terms of his own inimitable invention. Undertakers were, as I learned at once, the "Southern planters," the subjects of their ministrations the "people who are no longer with us," or, more directly, "deceasements." To fill the front-page weather ear was to "geese the doodlum," though "doodlum" was not to be confused with "didlum," which he reserved for the vacuities of public speakers, who "didn't say didlum"; and completing all copy, headlines, cutlines and layout for the front page or any other was to "saucer and blow" it, as in "When you have geesed the doodlum, please saucer and blow the front and send it to the little bald-headed bastard in heaven," i.e., to Odell Culler, the foreman of the composing room, on the floor directly above. An idle reporter was "fimmydiddling," generally on his "ambalaccus," while editorial writers were the "anointed ones." A story in which the management was known to take an interest was "sprinkled with holy water." A woman expecting a baby was "fragrant," and once delivered, a baby, including his own daughter, was a "papoose," who in turn gave birth to "grand papeese." When Frank Spencer underwent surgery, Nutt reported gleefully, "They had to survey and blast."

Opinions varied as to how he came by his argot—he maintained he'd borrowed much from Hobble McMichael—but his names for staffers were always his own. Frank Clingman, whose city desk sat next to his, was

"Clink" in address, "Herr Clingman" when spoken of, but Frank Spencer was not only "Cooch" under all circumstances but the fount and cause of "Coochism," which was anything Nutt wanted to deride that day. Jim Rush, facing him from the slot of the copy desk, was "Marse Jeems," no doubt in recognition of his aristocratic bearing, while George Thomas, a rim man of notorious awkwardness and confused appearance, was "Gorgeous George." Mark Ethridge, who'd written thousands of words reporting the 1948 North Carolina epidemic of infantile paralysis, inevitably became "Marco Polio," and Roy Thompson, for less evident reasons, was "Egghead." Hoke Norris quickly became "Hocus Pocus," though it would have been difficult to find a man less mysterious, and Bill Woestendiek, who was large, was "Wee Willie." Red Whitener, the late man on the copy desk, who lived in the country and grew vegetables he distributed generously all summer, thereby became "the Agrarian," while I, for reasons already only too apparent, was soon answering to "the Bald One." There was little chance of escaping Nutt's relentless nicknaming—even his wife, Margaret, had to go by "Fats," or sometimes "Mrs. Heavy"—and the few whose embarrassing luck it was to have to be called by their Christian names were either too obscure, too faceless or too briefly on staff to catch his attention. As Porter Dunlap, who brought the nightly "Sloppy Shoppe" of soft drinks to the newsroom, remarked, "That Mr. Caldwell, he takes all the misery out of the world."

Nutt frequently called Frank Spencer his "ex-Christian friend," as he did nearly everyone sooner or later, but Spencer was neither the original "ex-Christian friend," whose identity no one knew, nor the hopeless buffoon Nutt enjoyed painting him. He was Nutt's straw man, as Nutt was his, and they clearly adored each other beneath their perpetual raillery, the two halves of which had become a single comic turn, for though each was funnier than almost anyone else their comedy gained geometrically when they could play their wisecracks off each other. Spencer—"Cooch" universally, though Nutt preferred to spell it "Kooch"—was a local boy, the son of a prominent Winston-Salem physician, and had all but grown up on the *Journal*, since his mother had been the women's editor in the old days before it was merged with the *Sentinel*. Nutt sometimes argued that Cooch had been born on the premises, or found under a cabbage left at the door, but he also claimed that Spencer was so old that while serving as a cavalryman in the Civil War "they had to paint him purple so they could tell him from a horse."

Cooch's plentiful hair was white and his girth great, but in fact he was younger than Nutt. They'd been reporters together during the late 1920s, but then Cooch drifted over into sports, soon becoming sports editor and "the dean of North Carolina sportswriters," as the *Journal* often boasted, while Nutt settled into the news side. That—and the resulting placement of their desks at opposite ends of the newsroom—suited both perfectly: their endless jokes at each other's expense could be fired over the heads of both news and sports staffs, their favorite audience, and no ounce of derision lost.

The only hitch was that Cooch's hours were so erratic Nutt could never be sure he'd be there to receive his latest jape. Spencer was a nomad and a night owl who did everything, including his work, in his own odd way, from covering the home and away games of the baseball farm team presently in residence (Nutt called them "Cooch's Bums") to putting on the *Journal & Sentinel*'s annual high-school basketball tournament. His desk was so deep in unanswered letters, unfinished columns, notes for unwritten stories and reminders to call so-and-so that his typewriter was usually hard to find, and most of the nightly routine—incoming stories, wire-service statistics, editing and makeup—was supervised by his various underlings, who rarely knew where he was either. But his copy was professional and accurate and always in hand, even when Cooch had to call it in from East Bend or North Wilkesboro, by deadline. He loved, like the small boy he never ceased to be, to chase fire trucks and ride around half the night with cops; and the story was told that when he once got home at 3:00 A.M. his children assumed dawn had broken and began to dress for school. Nor could anyone forget the night he bellowed happily across the newsroom, "Hobble, I'm going to be a poppa!"—or McMichael's deliberate, deadpan reply: "Well, Cooch, all I can say is you've got some mighty nice neighbors."

Cooch's trademark greeting on all occasions, to intimates or strangers, in the flesh or on the phone, was "How's your liver?"—a foolproof means of controlling all conversation within the immediate area, especially among people unfamiliar with his greeting. He lost control, however, on Carl Wiegold's first day at the office: Wiegold, a photographer, was trotted up to be introduced and when asked the famous question launched solemnly into a long medical description of his own liver problems, including a number of clinical details, that left Cooch, for perhaps the only time in his life, dumbfounded. Later, with Wiegold safely out on assignment, he confided to Nutt that he wondered if the new photographer mightn't be "a little crazy. He's a hypochondriac."

Out of his genial wildness Cooch, like Nutt, had created a persona that was cunning and outrageous, and by the time I reached the *Journal* they'd both molded and polished themselves into legends for which the paper itself was famous. Like great actors they were never out of character, and together—our Estragon and Vladimir—they performed each evening a cheerfully inverted version of *Waiting for Godot*, a cranky duet of comic sanity in a world otherwise clearly mad.

22

By the spring of 1950 I'd gained enough experience and developed enough confidence in my skills to feel I could tackle more or less anything. Though no one had ever accused me of lacking self-confidence, eight or nine months on the *Journal* had deepened my sense that I was doing well at work for which I was especially suited; but there remained much—if not much I wanted to admit to—outside both my range and my narrative gift. The tutelage of Jim Rush, Frank Clingman and Worth Bacon had sharpened my copy, however, and the perpetual hullabaloo of Nutt Caldwell's newsroom, his worldly wisdom and in particular his uncanny if unsentimental knowledge of the community and its people had broadened my grasp of the news itself. It did not hurt that I had grown up in Winston-Salem and knew my way around—the kind of reflexive acquaintance with places and names I might otherwise have taken years to master, or might never have acquired; I had much of the city and surrounding area at my fingertips, remembered who lived on which side of what street and was a cousin of whom, and what was dim I could clarify with a word or two from Nutt. This was my good luck, and it did not go unnoticed or wasted. Years later Nutt remembered that I was one of the few staffers who could pick his way through almost any neighborhood in town.

Sooner or later I came close to doing so. Buena Vista, West Highlands, Ardmore, Salem, Southside, Bon Air and West End were neighborhoods in which I'd had school friends, or where I'd caught flies for Yale, and I rarely got lost in them; only in East Winston, the large Negro slum between downtown and City Hospital, was I ill at ease, and right to be. I covered a bit of everything. Though all of us had the primary responsibility of the news on our beats, at night, once the day's routine copy was written, each of us, unless committed to an evening function stemming from his beat, became available for general assignment, could be called on by Clingman or Nutt to tackle whatever came up on the spur of the moment. Much of the time this proved routine too— late obits, minor stories called in by stringers in East Bend or Walnut Cove—but often enough the evening brought bigger stuff: fires, shootings, on one occasion a dinner meeting at the Hotel Robert E. Lee announcing the formation of a group of prominent citizens to plan, finance and undertake the long-range preservation and restoration of Old Salem, which, as the city's founding site, core and soul, was a place as dear to my childhood as "Old Virginny" in the popular song; it gave me great pleasure to realize in subsequent decades that I'd been present, however modestly, at the creation. A similar occasion a few months later—though one in which I took more ambivalent pride—announced plans for the construction of something called a "shopping center," Winston-Salem's first but by no means its last.

A community improvement in which I could claim I had played a real, even substantial part had its origin in a series of stories I wrote that spring. Winston-Salem's support of cultural institutions was conspicuously greater than that of either its neighboring or indeed most American cities of comparable size, thanks to both the visionary philanthropy of its tobacco, textile and banking leadership and a relatively enlightened populace, which together had given it music, art and theatre of distinction; but in one respect it was laggard. Since before World War I its public library had been housed in a tiny downtown building, given by Andrew Carnegie, that the community itself had long since outgrown. The building had charm and was conveniently located, but its collection was meager and cramped and its staff of elderly women, though helpful, was hopelessly untrained in modern library technology. I had grown up using it and probably came close to knowing where 90 percent of its holdings were; but experience of a major university library, not to mention Baltimore's great Enoch Pratt Library, had shown me how central a good public library was to a thriving community. The problem was clear and the solution obvious: the city—and Forsyth County—needed a new library.

With a zeal I could not muster today I determined, with my bosses' approval, to undertake a series exposing the existing library's inadequacies; as a reporter I could not advocate its replacement, but surely that conclusion would be unavoidable. When I called Ralph Hanes, chairman of the library board and one of Winston-Salem's textile tycoons, I learned at once I need fear no resistance: he was as eager as I to persuade city and county fathers they must build and equip and greatly increase the funding of a new library; a series of stories stressing the shortcomings of the old institution would help him make his case, not only with governing bodies but with the wealthy men and women whose gifts would be crucial.

So many ambitions, public and private, come to nothing that the speed with which ours succeeded still takes my breath away. I wrote a sequence of four stories, spaced irregularly, detailing the old library's faults and contrasting them with the improvements, financial and material, Winston-Salem's peer North Carolina cities— Charlotte, Greensboro, Raleigh, Asheville—had been able to effect in recent years; my facts came largely from statistics provided by public sources and librarians: size of holdings, range of available reference materials, extent of use, funding, etc. I met no obstacle and heard no objection to what I was doing, least of all from the elderly staff, and the only "interference" I encountered at the paper came from Worth Bacon, whose extraordinary editing skill greatly improved my copy. No one complained to the *Journal* that I was a presumptuous upstart to criticize the wise men who ran the city and county or—unusual for me then and later—called for me to be tarred and feathered. For once I'd touched a nerve everyone in town seemed ready to quieten; and when Ralph Hanes went to the board of aldermen and county commissioners prepared to press them in his usual commanding way he found no need to demand anything. They agreed the library needed replacement, agreed they must do it at once and agreed to increase the library appropriation to match. What promised to be a donnybrook turned out to be a lovefeast. Ralph Hanes turned to the wealthy benefactors of earlier Winston-Salem cultural endeavors, who purred and paid. The ultimate moment came when his phone rang early one morning and Dick Reynolds, senior son of founding father R. J. Reynolds but a man who hadn't lived in Winston-Salem for years, told him that in honor of his wife's birthday he was donating the old Reynolds homesite on Fifth Street for the new library—an ideal location and an ideal conclusion to a happy story.

It was a dazzling experience and one from which I learned a lot: the power of facts; the power the press can exert even over those who believe they are immune to it; the undeniable truth that the people of the community had been taught they must pay for what they want, and would if properly persuaded. But perhaps what I cherished most for myself was none of these things but the respect and affection I'd developed for Ralph Hanes. My feeling for the plutocracy of Winston-Salem had always been, at best, grudging. They seemed to me handsome vulgarians who ruled wisely but arrogantly, and none more than he, who had struck me as a vainglorious stuffed shirt all too proud of his wealth, good looks and Yale degree. The Ralph Hanes I came to know was entirely different: opinionated and forceful, as became his intelligence, and rarely patient with fools, but willing to listen to others, to learn from them and work with them, and extraordinarily good at using his money, position and connections to bring about public betterment. He could bully his peers—I never heard a man demand and raise more money with a few telephone calls—but I never saw him bully anyone of more modest rank. No one ever called him humble, but his Arrow-collar look and patrician bearing overlay a man of genuine warmth and thoughtfulness capable of great public leadership and private kindness.

Few of my other stories—or adventures—were so consequential. Once, desperate for Sunday-feature material, I spent most of a week seeking out dangerous occupations and trying to perform them: washing office windows from an eighteenth-floor platform hanging from the Reynolds Building; riding in the sidecar of a police motorcycle weaving its way at sixty miles an hour through the clogged midday traffic of Fourth Street; raising my head through a manhole in the middle of Fifth; accompanying a platoon of cops on a raid in "The Pond," the city's worst slum, populated by thieves, pimps and whores, and waiting for the bullets to fly; riding a cropduster somewhere north of King among the rolling hills of the Sauratown Mountains. One cold morning, subbing for Roy Thompson, I drove to Boone to join a manhunt in the valleys and draws of the steeper, sharper Blue Ridge; I can still feel the damp, hear the dogs baying in the distance and overhear a nearby deputy mutter to no one, "Hell, nobody can survive up there more'n a day or two. He'll have to come out sooner or later." Bill Woestendiek and I roamed the city till dawn for most of two weeks tracking down night people, though when we'd finished our series, "While the City Sleeps," Frank Clingman thanked us solemnly, rolled it up and put it away in a drawer of the city desk, never to be seen again; we never learned why he wouldn't run it. A lighter moment was the evening Bill and I followed Tallulah Bankhead, who was appearing at the State Theatre in a road-company production of *Private Lives*, up Fifth Street to her hotel, only to be dismissed with a wave of her regal hand and the husky word, "Nothing." Mark Ethridge's headline was better than our story about why we got no story: "To the Press No One is Culah / Than Tempestuous Tallulah." Another comic note was struck when, after staying up all night to cover the Moravian Easter sunrise service, I asked Nutt Caldwell why it was necessary to send anyone to cover in person an event so unwavering and unalterable; his answer was succinct: "In case Bishop Pfohl steps out on the church porch, says, 'The Lord is risen,' and drops dead." Less comic was the Sunday night I covered a fire north of Danbury, found nothing left of the house but the glowing outline of its footings and took the facts from a woman, the owner, in the front seat of my car; later that night she and her lover were arrested and charged with murdering her husband by tying him to a chair and torching the place. That was the way disputes were often settled in Stokes County, Nutt said, offering the prediction, "They'll walk." They walked.

In all of this perpetual motion and excitement my pleasure was the delight of a small boy let loose with a box of matches in a fireworks factory. I wish I could claim, with appropriate gravity, that my stunts and pranks steadily deepened my understanding of the role of the press in furthering American democracy, that I began to learn that news occurs in a continuum of events from which it can be separated only at the price of distortion, that every story is part of a context; but—though I was innocent of malice—I rarely gave even a passing thought to the consequences of what I was doing, may never, in fact, have realized that what I was doing *had* consequences. I was not deliberately destructive; I took great pains to make my work accurate; but I was, a lot of the time, what today is called a "loose cannon." I loved sensation; I loved seeing my byline on the front page of the *Journal*, where it appeared with increasing regularity; I loved knowing a story of mine had disturbed the comfortable. Being a young newspaperman—having the freedom of a booming city, possessing the privilege of almost automatic access to its highest and lowest, being fully accepted as part of the liveliest, most stimulating and most irreverent company I had ever known—was, I suppose, the late adolescence I had lost to the war. I never knowingly felt I'd been cheated of the pleasures most young men experience in their late teens, yet the sense of deprivation must have been there, waiting to be corrected. Pounding the streets and a battered Royal upright for the *Journal* gave me what I'd missed, and I took it all: working harder than I had to because it never seemed like work; going everywhere at all hours and talking to all sorts of people for stories that rarely had much importance beyond broadening the range of my personal experience; writing, as I flattered myself, more and more clearly and concisely; reveling, above all, in the good humor of a friendly, funny newsroom in which every riposte, wisecrack or pun was instantly evaluated, occasionally applauded, more often derided but invariably repeated. Journalism can be a serious occupation, and some of the older hands must have realized it; but for me and the *Journal* companions of my generation it was simply the best fun on earth.

23

Then suddenly, as things will, things changed.

The outbreak of war in Korea was the first. All of us were hopelessly unprepared, both rationally and emotionally, and the news, clicking in on the AP and UP wires across the newsroom, struck us like a thunderbolt. Like most veterans of World War II we'd blinded ourselves to the perennial instability of our century, keeping the Cold War at arm's length with self-deceiving reassurances that the futile death and destruction we'd witnessed were unimaginable again, that our wartime friendships with the Soviet Union and China must surely transcend temporary postwar differences. A war against either was unthinkable, and the existence of the A-bomb made its effects unforeseeable. Nor could we anticipate whether or how war might affect us personally. The youngest of us,

Bill Woestendiek and I especially, wondered half-seriously if we'd be drafted again, though after a few weeks that anxiety was relieved by the publication of new classifications placing us beyond conscription because of the long times we'd already served. But he had an additional worry. The previous winter both of us had been courted by army intelligence to seek reserve commissions. I already had application papers I'd been given at Baltimore's Camp Holabird, where I'd been courted similarly my last year at Hopkins, but I'd never completed them. Bill had completed and submitted his and now awaited what seemed inevitable. He had a wife and daughter as well as nearly four years in the army air force during World War II, but now, to his anguish, he appeared to have made the classic army mistake of volunteering. In early fall he was called, commissioned in military intelligence and packed off, in a few weeks, to Japan, then Korea. Despite identical intentions I'd been too disorganized to send in my papers and was spared.

His departure left a hole in both the newsroom and my personal life, though by then the two were virtually the same; and the hole was deepened by the nearly simultaneous departure of Hoke Norris for a year at Harvard. The Nieman Fellowships were a prestigious and richly coveted honor, especially in an era when fellowships and scholarships of any kind were fewer than they eventually became, and for Hoke it was a chance not to be missed. He lacked outside means, and approaching forty he'd been a hardworking newsman, with time out for war, for fifteen years. He was the *Journal*'s most seasoned reporter and by far its supplest and most forceful writer, but he was also ambitious to write serious fiction and needed the guidance of experienced peers, something he was unlikely to find in Winston-Salem. So a free year at Harvard, where amongst interesting companions he'd be able to explore whatever academic byways he liked, was an important opportunity. But for me, who had come quickly to make him my wise mentor, the prospect of his absence as both colleague and friend was depressing.

The absences in my life had become a real problem, in fact, for I had invested much of myself in my friendships. Mark Ethridge was leaving for a job on the *Washington Post*. Bonnie Angelo, a lifelong friend and one of the liveliest members of our crowd, left for the *Richmond Times-Dispatch*. That spring I'd fallen besottedly in love with a striking senior at Salem College, a pianist of brilliant promise whose gypsy beauty and mercurial charm I found irresistible; my attachment to her was chaste but obsessively intense, and when she went off to graduate school, making it clear that the romance was over, I felt I'd collapse. Her decision was the right one, for our temperaments were poorly matched for anything as demanding as marriage, as eventually I realized; but love had never so *possessed* me, and losing her left me like a man broken on the wheel.

By then the Korean War was dominating everything, not only the news—war news almost overnight had swallowed the front page of the *Journal*—but public attention and conversation. The same surprise and skepticism so many of us at the paper had felt at its outbreak seemed to be nearly universal; nearly everyone knew someone called unexpectedly to duty, like Bill Woestendiek, and most of the men in town too young to have made World War II looked around them wondering when the blow would fall, as it soon did to Walt Friedenberg, my friend and colleague, who, commissioned and uniformed, found himself headed east; and though few expressed outright objection to Truman's intervention a persistent undercurrent of dissatisfaction with the war, especially so soon after the end of World War II, suggested clearly if not yet loudly that this would prove a widely unpopular conflict most Americans believed a wiser foreign policy could have prevented.

The departures of Hoke Norris and Bill Woestendiek made staff shifts inevitable, for their beats were the best and most demanding on the paper, and soon Rixie Hunter and I moved up to take their places, if not necessarily to fill their shoes. Almost at once I began to realize that at the courthouse I was in a new dimension of journalism. Even at the humblest level the institutions and actions of government are weightier than Rotary Club luncheons, the promotional schemes and triumphs of the chamber of commerce or even washing skyscraper windows eighteen stories up: they affect more lives more directly, and they do not vanish, to be replaced by another novelty, with the next edition. Through superior court, keystone of the North Carolina judicial system, there passed a daily cavalcade of cruelty, stupidity, anger and grief, or in alternate terms the frequently intractable disputes between citizen and corporation, citizen and citizen, corporation and corporation; the participants in such trials, whatever their outcome, would not soon recover. The clerk's office, beneath the big courtroom, bulged with the paper of other events and disturbances: births, deaths, marriages, divorces, damage and property suits. Across the hallway were the vaults of the register of deeds, where much of the future of the area could be foreseen, by those who knew how, in the records of land and other property transactions. Upstairs was the sheriff's office, a mysterious, generally secret world managed by Ernie Shore, once a big-league ballplayer and roommate of Babe Ruth who'd become, it seemed, a genial but permanent officeholder. The superintendent of schools was around the corner, as was the office of the county attorney. I got to know them all and became friends with a few, and from them I started to understand that public institutions are an infinitely extended, seamless web of connections and relationships, and that the "news" of them I reported daily in what my profession called "stories" was really only a series of units arbitrarily plucked, for literary purposes, from something too large and too complex to be wholly understood, let alone described, in the neater, more strictly organized accounts in which journalism specialized. Newspapers, as Dean Acheson once said of foreign policy, were "clearer than the truth."

Among the many others to whom I became attached on the courthouse beat, all as friends or sources and occasionally both, were the lawyers and politicians whose natural habitat it was as surely as mine was the *Journal* newsroom. In those days Southern politics was still essentially a thing of local machines—though we called them "organizations"—dominating local affairs on behalf of the larger machines in the various state capitals; they functioned, in North Carolina as everywhere else, out of the courthouses, and little happened of significance that lacked the imprimatur of the big boys at the center of the numerous webs the legislatures had spun to ensure their own control. Because of the power of the Reynolds Tobacco Company, the several Hanes textile companies and the Wachovia Bank and Trust Company, however, Winston-Salem and Forsyth County boasted countervailing forces most poorer sections of the state lacked; and the political scene at the courthouse was always one of tensions relieved only when compromises on taxes, appropriations and appointments were finally reached between the "nineteenth floor"— i.e., Reynolds headquarters—and Raleigh. The local lawyers and pols, many of whom were officeholders or party leaders, were always hard at work wheeling and dealing on such issues, though for me it was hard to see, once I understood a little of how things worked, how what they did mattered as long as the "nineteenth floor" made all the final decisions. This was still the era of cigars, spittoons and lobbies reeking of Lysol, so the atmosphere was fragrant, but I came to like—if not always admire—most of the courthouse crowd. Almost all were bright, quick, funny and as cynical as the scruffiest newspaperman, and I could trust few unless their interest in the truth was clear; but they were the same sort of good company as the flotsam who populated and passed through the newsroom, good-humored, good at telling stories, never ordinary, and it was impossible not to enjoy them. Those who appeared in court were actors of superior talent, and the big-time corporate lawyers who rarely had to soil themselves with the cigar smoke were skillful at assembling complex facts and arguments; and a tiny few, most notably Irving Carlyle, who was also a state senator, boasted intellectual gifts that would have honored any university.

These were the things—the people, the policies, the relationships, the connections—by which I began to broaden my understanding of journalism and of the larger society of which it was, to the distress of many, so increasingly conspicuous a part. Seeing past the mere fun of daily reporting was a change, and another came that winter when Worth Bacon acceded to my request for a few months on the copy desk. Unlike many of my friends I had no wish to rise to news executive, nor any interest in becoming a permanent copyeditor; my professional ambitions were wholly literary and focused on reporting and writing. But I had developed a profound respect for the skill with which Jim Rush and others could, by shifting a sentence here and adding a transition there, by cutting and rearranging, untangle and condense copy and by doing so turn a mediocre story into an interesting, coherent and sometimes even an exciting one; and, no doubt selfishly, I wanted to learn how to do it myself. I took my place on the rim to Jim Rush's right and was soon up to my neck in wire-service copy, trimming it to specific length, sometimes combining AP and UP versions of the same story, learning to compose headlines on the typewriter—a demanding task at the *Journal*, where a "head" not only had to fit the space a story's size permitted but in doing so must satisfy such special rules as forbade splitting an infinitive or separating a preposition from its object or a noun from its modifier across two lines, not to mention Jim Rush's fastidious dislike of slang, jargon and triteness or his insistence that the two or three lines of a "head" be of similar length. This sort of finicky attention to the smallest detail was characteristic of the *Journal*'s overall high standards of presentation, and it made every page of the paper extraordinarily orderly, neat and easy to read; but it took concentration and patience to master, for it was a form of high craftsmanship, and I came, in learning it, to admire and to try ever after to emulate it. I was especially and immensely proud of the job I was given to do when General MacArthur, sacked by Truman, returned to testify before an angry Congress; the daily reporting of the hearing was long and far more detailed than the *Journal* had space for, and I had the task of cutting and compressing—but not distorting—the teletype copy to the numerous but still limited columns Worth Bacon had allotted. It took several hours each afternoon and evening to get that day's story trimmed and shaped, for I found I had to go back to the top again and again, as I cut, to ensure I was giving a fair version of the facts; but it was, I suppose, the most instructive editing assignment I ever undertook.

Though less dramatic, a more momentous portent of radical change in my world came, while I was still on the copy desk, with the AP's initiation of teletypesetter service. Till then technology had required that all incoming wire-service copy be edited by the member paper, then set into type by local Linotype operators. This was cumbersome and took time, but it also allowed a broad range of editing choices as to length, emphasis, typeface, type size and column width; and, since wire copy arrived entirely in capital letters, it necessitated—but also allowed—a member paper to impose its own stylistic requirements. For a paper as fussy as the *Journal* was about capitalization, abbreviation and punctuation this gave it the chance to see that wire copy met its own standards of order and clarity; and it was an opportunity purists like the *Journal*'s treasured. At one blow teletypesetting destroyed it. AP copy now arrived on a punched tape that when fitted to a Linotype set the type automatically; this saved labor costs but meant that wire copy now bore the AP's style, not ours. For a few months Jim Rush and the rest of us struggled to correct especially grievous violations of the *Journal* stylebook, but this too proved awkward and expensive, and soon we contented ourselves with cutting and rearranging; and not long afterward, in the interest of internal consistency, the style of local copy was brought into line with the AP's. Presently the introduction of AP Wirephoto and then other forms of automation, all of which undeniably increased the efficiency of newspaper production, presaged the mounting centralization and standardization of the American press that continue today with computerized transmission and composition. Abundant color and the varied employment of graphics are a boon, of course, but they come at the cost of the regional and local character, flavor and look that most newspapers once boasted. The *Journal*, delicate, cranky and often pedantic about small matters—it was "*the* Rev. John Doe," not "Rev. John Doe," thereafter "the Rev. Mr. Doe," not "Rev. Doe"—lost something precious and irrecoverable to progress.

24

During the summer of 1950 I'd written a story that attracted attention beyond the immediate range of the
Journal. One of the polio epidemics that periodically
plagued the nation broke out in Virginia, particularly in
the strip of southwestern Virginia slightly northwest of
Winston-Salem. The toll was heavy; larger Virginia hospitals able to cope with it mobilized in Roanoke and
Richmond, necessitating elaborate evacuation efforts;
and no community was harder hit than the small town of
Wytheville. No outside reporter had gone into Wytheville to observe what was happening there firsthand,
however, and that silence aroused my curiosity, already
activated by army experience in epidemiology and a
summer job assisting, though at a humble level, in polio
research. Wytheville was well outside *Journal* circulation

or ordinary coverage but less than a hundred miles distant, and when I proposed to have a look there Worth Bacon and Frank Clingman quickly agreed.

Photographer Frank Jones and I packed drinking water and a hamper of sandwiches, which in the absence of dependable scientific knowledge of how polio was transmitted seemed prudent, and set off. Wytheville seemed a ghost town: empty streets, empty filling stations, empty stores; no one could have doubted that something was seriously amiss, and the fear we sensed was wholly understandable. I talked at length with the public-health officer for the area, who had a huge map on the wall behind his desk bearing pins showing where cases had occurred, and with his exhausted nurses; Jones took a lot of pictures, and on the main drag we tried to talk with a couple of the handful of people daring to go out, but they refused us brusquely, suspicious, no doubt, that we might carry the polio bug ourselves; and the people at the local weekly were equally unforthcoming. It was a spooky place, and having done what we could we drove home. The story appeared a few days later in the Sunday paper, well-displayed but by no means overplayed, and instead of sensational it was subdued.

I thought that was the end of it; but the fact that no other reporter, from Virginia or anywhere else, had gone into Wytheville made interest in my account higher than I would have expected. It began to show a few days later when other papers began to reprint my story, still bearing my byline but without *Journal* permission, something so commonplace I thought nothing of it. But then two big papers reprinted it too, prominently, and had the courtesy not only to give me credit but to send small checks as payment: the *Washington Post* and the *Richmond Times-Dispatch*. A few days after that John Colburn, managing editor of the latter, offered me a job there, and Peyton Winfree, executive editor of the *Lynchburg News & Advance*, invited me to be his telegraph editor. I was flattered but still unready to move. I had no desire to become a telegraph editor and Lynchburg was considerably smaller than Winston-Salem; but the *Times-Dispatch* was a big step up in an era when an ambitious young Southern reporter's way to the *New York Times* or *Herald-Tribune* lay through apprenticeship in Richmond, Atlanta or Nashville. I asked Colburn to give me a year's rain check, and he generously assured me he'd have a spot for me when I wanted it.

I had sound reasons for staying and was glad afterward I had. With only a year's experience I needed seasoning. I did not want to leave the *Journal* just when its two ablest reporters were away on leave. I loved the work and the people I worked with and was unready to loosen that tie. Above all, however, I sensed I ought to remain

awhile longer with my parents. I am far from super-
stitious and claim no premonition I could have articulated. Between 1942 and my graduation in 1949 I'd seen
little of them. College, then war, then college again had
separated us; and though I'd spent most of my summers
at home I'd been home only technically: to eat, sleep
and shower before roistering off to another date, another
tennis match, another evening drinking beer with
friends. My upside-down hours at the *Journal* were little
better, but at least I saw them at dinner and often on
Sundays, when, after they returned from church and
before I went to work, we had a drink and dinner together at the Forsyth Country Club. I did not pay them
anything like the attention they deserved and took their
hospitality for granted, but I began to enjoy their company in the new way parents and children must find as
they grow older. They knew and understood a lot more
than I'd realized; they were an invaluable source, after
thirty years in Winston-Salem, on who was who, and
what, where and how the city worked, and I drew heav-
ily on their knowledge and wisdom. Besides, their pride
in my good start in the world was obvious; and even their
efforts to make me assume a few adult responsibilities—
opening a checking account, buying a car of my own,
paying a nominal sum for my room and board—were
made so gently I usually ended by imagining I'd thought
of them myself.

Yet it was clear, even to me, that we had reached a major turning point in our lives. My sister Anne, though two years younger, had graduated from Converse in 1948, gone to graduate school at Tulane, come home to be married in 1950 and returned with her husband to New Orleans. I was on the brink of some similar and equally fundamental move, though I did not know what or when or where it would be. What we all faced was inevitable and healthy but painful to contemplate. A successfully functioning family is a mystery I do not pretend to have pierced, but it was clear to us that ours had come, as families do, to a moment when everything— home, roles, our relationships to one another—must change forever.

Inevitable though it was, it changed suddenly. One day in June I was instructed to haul myself to the police station at city hall: Roy Thompson had taken a new assignment as a features specialist and regular "personality" columnist, something new for the *Journal*, and I was to take over the police beat. The hours were even worse than before, five till two, but I reveled in the prospect, for I'd wanted to cover the cops regularly from the start and still had a small boy's zest for chasing fire trucks, besides which I'd have a full day of leisure when everyone else was pursuing normal working hours. The country-club pool had never been less crowded.

It lasted only a few weeks. I was at the police station

when Frank Clingman called to say there was an emergency at my parents'. There I found my father lying on the dining-room floor, in great pain, and an ambulance waiting at the curb. His doctor assured me it "might" be indigestion, but I had seen and read enough to know that his pallor and sweating almost certainly meant he'd suffered a heart attack. I stayed with him at City Hospital through the night, and early next morning they moved him to a private room upstairs. By the time an electrocardiogram confirmed the heart attack he had slipped into unconsciousness, from which he never awoke.

He lingered five days, very pale, very still, the slow rise and fall of his chest the sole sign that he was alive. Both the doctor and the hospital did what could be done; but coronary-care units were still more than a decade away, as were the drugs now employed routinely to sustain the victims of acute myocardial infarction during the crucial first week after onset, and the conventional treatment remained, in essence, bed rest and nursing. The paper was generous about my time at the hospital; my detective friends vigorously tracked down private-duty nurses; one of the nurses I'd known the year before at the County Hospital volunteered. Almost everyone in Winston-Salem seemed to know him and love him and offered to help.

I loved him too, with the wild, uncritical adoration a son can form for a father whose virtues he knows he lacks himself and is unlikely ever to acquire. In my eyes he was perfect, perfectly integrated; and forty years later I continue to believe so. He had never raised his hand and rarely his voice to punish or admonish me, a boy whose self-absorption, carelessness and apparent indifference to others must have strained his patience. But patience he had, the unwavering manifestation of his essential inner calm, and he had much else besides: affection, kindness, generosity, empathy, magnanimity, restraint—the knightly virtues that made him *sans peur et sans reproche*. He was cheerful, optimistic. He believed, as his son could not, in the great Victorian abstractions: Progress, Democracy, the Goodness of Man. With the Presbyterian church and the Democratic party as his pillars, he accepted the simple faith that America could do anything, solve any problem, surmount any obstacle. In this he was like most of his generation, and the sunniness of his confidence gave him strength and certainty.

I loved him and took him shamelessly for granted. Knowing he would be there anyway, I neglected to talk with him, though he was the easiest company I knew, and it had never occurred to me that he was not immortal. It had been a year of family deaths—his brother William, Mother's brother James—but I'd refused to see in them that he was vulnerable too. He was sixty-four, his bearing soldierly, his step gallant; his face was still classically chiseled, his features firm; he was never sick, never absent, and because he was so steadfast I had enjoyed a long boyhood of great privilege and good fortune, even my war having proved lucky.

The last night was hot and damp, the hospital without air conditioning. I remained at his bedside through the small hours as he slipped into his final moments. Somewhere Freud proposes that a boy becomes a man only when his father's death brings down upon him the full weight of adult life. I felt that weight descending as his breathing became shallow. Just before dawn the nurse went down the hall to summon my mother, who got there barely in time, gray with exhaustion and grief. I held my father's hand and put my other arm around her, unable to imagine that she too would die, of the same disease and even younger than he, fifteen months later. An intern, whom I remembered from high school, came and injected caffeine directly into my father's chest. A moment later a single shuddering sound issued from his throat and his heart ceased to beat.

The sun had risen by the time we left the hospital for the parking lot, but the downtown streets were empty. I drove my mother home, where a cluster of their friends were waiting, and was a boy no more.